I USED TO HAVE A HANDLE ON LIFE BUT IT BROKE

MARY LOVERDE

Six Power Solutions for Women with Too Much to Do

A Fireside Book
Published by Simon & Schuster

New York   London   Toronto   Sydney   Singapore

FIRESIDE
Rockefeller Center
1230 Avenue of the Americas
New York, NY 10020

FIRESIDE and colophon are registered trademarks of Simon & Schuster, Inc.

For information regarding special discounts for bulk purchases,
please contact Simon & Schuster Special Sales:
1-800-456-6798 or business@simonandschuster.com

Designed by Lisa Stokes

Manufactured in the United States of America

10   9   8   7   6   5   4   3   2

Library of Congress Cataloging-in-Publication Data is available.

ISBN 0-684-85419-8

Acknowledgment is made of the following material: Page 46, quotation from verse of Kym Croft Miller, copyright © 2000 by Kym Croft Miller (used by permission of author). Page 66, cartoon, courtesy of *Non Sequitur,* © Wiley Miller (distributed by Universal Press Syndicate; reprinted with permission; all rights reserved). Pages 132–34, quotation from *A Grace Disguised,* by Gerald Sittser, © 1995 by Gerald Sittser (used by permission of Zondervan). Pages 140 and 149, cartoons, courtesy of *Frank & Ernest,* © 1996 and 1998 by Thaves (reprinted with permission; newspaper distribution by NEA, Inc.). Page 157, cartoon, courtesy of *In the Bleachers,* © 1999 by Steve Moore (reprinted with permission of Universal Press Syndicate; all rights reserved).

ACKNOWLEDGMENTS

I had to take my own advice and let go to write this book. Special thanks to all those who helped me power up!

Robert Miller, a true friend in every sense of the word. Thanks for supporting me and for always filling me with energy.

Jillian Manus, my savvy, brilliant, and kind agent. How lucky can a writer be to have an agent like you?

Caroline Sutton, my editor. I am forever grateful for the calm confidence you instill in me and the literary talent you brought to this project. You are a joy to work with.

Kym Miller, my energetic friend. You have ingenious ideas and a generous spirit. Thanks for your tremendous contributions to this book.

Jaye Lunsford, the thinker. Your probing thoughts and unique angles on the topic helped this book take shape. I am sure Lillian had her hand in this too, and I am grateful to both of you.

Annette Simmons, my storytelling genius. Thanks for your wonderful gifts that inspire us all.

LeAnn Thieman, my ever supportive friend. You taught me so much about writing and editing. Thanks for the countless hours you spent on my project in the middle of your own deadlines. I will enjoy seeing you soar.

Sam Horn, my imaginative friend. We need to figure out how to clone you. Every author needs a Sam Horn sitting at the desk, ready to brainstorm at a moment's notice.

Lynn Price, a true visionary. I admire your single-minded goodness and am honored to travel the path together.

Lou and Jonellen Heckler, the good guys. You will never know how much you influence me every day and how grateful I am for your mentoring.

Rolf and Mary Benirschke, my role models. Our chance meeting twelve years ago changed the course of my life.

Monicah McGee, Diane Butler, Diane Sieg, Shelly Humbach, Anne Taylor, Jennifer Schulte, and Chris Roules, my readers. I am forever indebted for your taking time out of your busy schedules to participate in discussion groups and read draft after draft and give invaluable feedback.

Christy Hughes and Barbara Lubbers, my loving friends. You challenged and stretched me and cared enough to be honest and guide me to a clearer understanding. This book would not be possible without you.

Kym Davick, a light in my life. Thanks for encouraging me to "go deep" and for surrounding me with inspiring beauty.

Doug Wiermaa, my friend and confidant. Thanks for always getting me to the church on time.

Mary Jones, the inventive one. Thanks for believing in me and always supporting my dreams.

Scott Friedman, Mark Sanborn, and Eric Chester, members of my mastermind group. I am honored to be in the midst of your collective genius.

To all my friends from around the globe who phone and send me letters and e-mails that keep me connected to real life.

Melanie Mills, my sensitive friend. You always remind me of the importance of my soul.

Brenda Abdilla, my cherished champion. What joy, energy, and love you bring to my life!

And most of all, special thanks to Joe, Sarah, Emily, and Nicholas. I love you with all my heart!

To my mother, Lou Schulte, the most powerful woman I know,
and to my daughters, Sarah and Emily,
who are becoming powerful women

CONTENTS

CONTENTS

12

PREFACE

Dear Readers,

Women are powerful. Through the ages, Joan of Arc, Rosa Parks, Indira Gandhi, Eleanor Roosevelt, Madame Curie, and other pioneers have created role models and paths for us to follow. And now, according to futurists and cultural anthropologists, a critical mass of educated, experienced, and economically stable women worldwide stands poised to wield their power with a force and duration this world has never before seen.

Katie, bar the door, here we come.

The generation of women who marched for their causes while they burned their bras, bumped their heads on the glass ceiling, and then successfully took their bruised noggins into business for themselves and fought for rights and corrected many wrongs—these are the women who are leading the way. Equally powerful will be the next generations of females, who've benefited and learned from their older sisters. Their passion, global view, and innovative approaches will create an explosion of healing change that only a group of women who have mastered the Internet and mosh pits alike can cause.

Many of us sense the change coming. I have seen an ever-growing grassroots movement of women wanting to know more about their power. I experienced this firsthand when I attended a Powerful Woman's weekend retreat in 2000 in Greensboro, North Carolina. Annette Simmons, author of *The Story Factor* and *Territorial Games*, gathered fifteen women, from NASA researchers to artists, diverse in age, race, and opinion, who spent two days sharing their stories of power.

I was struck by Annette's opening welcome. She said, "I am a powerful woman. I don't know how I got this way. I have no idea what it is about me that makes me so powerful. I actually understand masculine power—mainly winning—better than feminine power. Still, I know that the world needs our feminine power to re-balance itself and heal the suffering."

I believe she is right. The world does need our feminine power. It's time for us to understand what we do to block our power and what we can do to maximize it by identifying the behaviors that will get us what we need and want.

This book is one step in that direction. Thank you for taking this journey with me.

Warmly,

Mary LoVerde

ONE

Getting a Grip

GIVE IT UP
Controlling Our Lives

IF ONLY I COULD get a handle on my life. Then I'd finally be able to have some time for myself, the kids, and my husband. I'd read the stack of books on my nightstand, put the piles of photos sitting in their envelopes in albums, and cook healthy meals. If I could just get a grip, I'd solve the problems at work, keep a cleaner house, and pay more attention to my aging parents. With just a little more leverage over my life, I could run the cat to the vet, the kids to dance and debate practice, and the tax forms to the IRS. I could volunteer more. I could lose weight, I could . . . well, you know, if I could just get control . . .

As women, we feel responsible for just about everything. And when we put "everything" on a to-do list, it makes for a very full day. As a result, we are exhausted, overwhelmed, and inundated, with no relief in sight. We tried to solve the too-much-to-do-not-enough-time-to-do-it problem by going faster, and now even at warp speed, we're getting further behind. A law of physics tells us that it takes four times as much energy to go twice as fast. No wonder we're tired.

Even those superwomen who can fly faster than a speeding minivan recognize that rushing no longer works. So we have switched gears. Our new favorite strategy is to "simply" get a handle on it all. Yes, yes, that's it! If only we could be in charge, get a grip, *gain control* of the situation, then we could finally live the good life.

I wondered if this new approach was working, so I began to observe women I believed were successful. I heard Linda Ellerbee, TV journalist and author, deliver an insightful, witty speech detailing her life as a divorcee, mother of two children, recovering alcoholic, and breast cancer survivor. She regaled us with tales of her firings, her career moves, and her leap of faith when she (against conventional wisdom) started her own company, Lucky Duck Productions. Then she said one line, and I didn't hear another word she said: "If I had predicted at any given moment in my life what I would be doing in the next five years, I would have been wrong 100 percent of the time."

My brain froze. Here was a tremendously respected and accomplished woman who used her power to get what she wanted in life, and yet she knew her success was not due to having a firm grip on what would happen next. She held no illusions that she was in control and seemed very comfortable with that truth.

I was intrigued and filled with hope. I reasoned that perhaps I too have enough power to get what I want in my life without forcing, pushing, and obsessing. Maybe getting a handle on my life isn't the answer.

I became very curious about the concept of control and the role it plays in our lives. Does striving for control help or hinder us? Does anyone ever really get control, and if so, what is the price? Do I need to be in control of my life to live the way I want to? What does control have to do with being a powerful woman? I read books, interviewed women from all walks of life from around the world, conducted focus groups, led seminars, and listened at dinner parties. Here's what I learned about control.

We Say We Want Control

Our language suggests that control is a big deal. I've listened to how we describe ourselves when we are out of balance. Women talk a lot about their need for control. Rarely do I get through an entire conversation without hearing something about it:

"As soon as I get things under control . . ." This is an odd phrase when you think about it. What things? Under where?

"I've got to get on top of things . . ." "I've got to get to the bottom of this . . ." We are very busy swarming around. How can we be on both the top and the bottom of everything?

"I need to get it nailed down." One of my friends quipped in reply: "I nailed it once; I just can't remember what I nailed it *to*."

"I've got a death grip on it, and it is still beyond my control!" "Death grip" is a telling phrase.

When a culture has an important concept, it creates many words to describe it. You may have heard that the Eskimos have a hundred words for snow. Well, if the number of descriptive words is any reflection, control plays a big role in our lives. Our language has everything from birth and mind control to nuclear arms and gun control. Use the word *control*, and nearly everyone has a strong opinion and is ready and willing to share it.

We're supposed to control our distractions, our dogs, and our dandruff. We want controlling interest. We're incensed when parents won't control their kids, and just watch what happens to some people when they can't find the remote control. Think of a life without control-top panty hose. There is no question about it: We want control!

Research Supports My Hypothesis

Our intense desire for control is not something I dreamed up. Yankelovich, Inc., one of the premiere national marketing research firms, reports that throughout most of the 1990s, the consumer's emphasis was on control. For example, eight out of ten women agreed with the statement, "It's important to me to feel in charge of each and every part of my life," and six out of ten women agreed with the statement, "Lately I find I'm looking for ways of getting more control over my life."

Yankelovich, Inc., even created a framework for understanding how we deal with control, which they called Strategic Control. Within this framework, we use three main strategies:

Jettison things that simply aren't important, or at least not worth the effort.

Delegate those things that can be delegated.

Control those things that remain.

According to their research, consumers were not, in the last decade, inclined to jettison (let go of anything), "as notions of 'sacrifice' and 'compromise' were increasingly unacceptable. Given a fundamental lack of trust, delegation was equally difficult. The results: massive 'to-do' lists and high stress levels."

But a ray of hope shines through. A new pattern is emerging—an improved approach to managing tasks in our lives and, more important, managing our most precious resources: time and energy. I smiled when I read that the Yankelovich researchers have called the new approach "lightening up," which means, in part, not overanalyzing every decision and instead putting a continuing focus on our quality of life *now* and a decreased focus on accomplishments and duty. Perhaps we are ready to learn a new way.

Women *Are* Different

As we begin to adapt new strategies and tap into our feminine powers, we must understand that women belong to a special club. Control is often perceived as a male issue, but women have a unique perspective on it. We deal with stress and the feelings of responsibility differently from men because we react to a wider range of outside stressors. We have more on our plate and therefore more control issues. Ronald Kessler, professor of health care policy at Harvard Medical School, asked 166 married couples to keep a daily stress diary for six weeks. He found women feel stress more often because they take a more holistic view (or is it "whole-list-ic view?") of everyday life. "A man may worry if some-one in his immediate family is sick; his wife takes on the burdens of the whole neighborhood. Men take care of one thing [at a time]," he says. "Women put the pieces together."

I know just what he means. I go to bed at night worrying about the starving children who need my leftovers. I lie awake mentally rehearsing the four things I did not get done (and are therefore out of my control) and ignore the 4,752 things I did do. I try to figure out how my friend can save her marriage, my kids can learn the value of money, and we can get the filmmakers to decrease violence. By 2:00 A.M. I'm trying to solve the trillion-dollar national debt and the Middle East peace crisis. My nights are busy.

One day I got this anonymous fax:

MEMO FROM GOD:
Do not feel totally, personally, irrevocably responsible for everything. That's My job.

I never did find out who faxed it, but apparently the sender thought I was taking this control issue just a little too far. I *do* feel totally responsible for everything. This is, of course, a heavy, and impossible, burden. I can't remember who told me the load was mine to carry, but I spend enormous amounts of energy, countless hours, and an infinite number of tears trying to control the things I cannot control. Most women I talk to feel the same. When I ask them about life balance issues, I always hear the same word: *control.*

Our Feminine Circuitry Predisposes Us

My female-wired brain is responsible for this nocturnal flight of ideas. Unlike men with their unifocus, I've got, just like the song says, "the whole wide world in my hands." Helen Fischer, an anthropologist at Rutgers University and author of *The First Sex,* writes that compared to men, women "tend to gather more data that pertain to a topic and connect these details faster. As women make decisions, they weigh more variables, consider more options and outcomes, recall more points of view, and see more ways to proceed. They integrate, generalize, and synthesize." Perhaps that explains why my husband can sleep so peacefully beside me while I ponder the problems of the universe.

The Difference Isn't Black and White; It's Gray and White

I am fascinated with the breakthrough research in neuroscience that suggests explanations for our different abilities. Compared to men, it's not just our hips that are bigger. Our prefrontal cortexes (where we organize thoughts and can think contextually) are larger, and the bridges that connect the right and left hemispheres of our brains, the corpus callosum and the anterior commissure, are both significantly larger too. When we solve problems, different parts of our gray and white matter fire up. Our neurons are more densely packed in some areas than they are in the male brain. We use both sides of our brain for talking, giving us the linguistic edge over men. Our senses of touch, smell, vision, taste, and hearing are all more finely tuned. So when we're told to "use our brain," we really do, even more so than men.

By neurological design, women are uniquely physiologically, genetically, and psychologically well equipped to use the strategy of control. But a strength overused can become a weakness. As I will show you in the following chapters, our natural talents sometimes feed our urge to control in ways far different from men. We multitask until we drop because our brains will. We may overnurture our children because our neurons respond more intensely to emotion. Long-term planning is a function of our larger, highly efficient prefrontal cortex, so controlling the future sounds reasonable to us. But our innate tendencies don't have to get us into trouble. As we will learn, there's a better way than striving for control to get what we want.

We Control Out of the Goodness of Our Hearts

I was convinced about our gender's desire for some sense of control the day I received this e-mail from my friend who is married, the mother of a one year old, and an entrepreneur. She is wildly successful in all of her roles but exhausted from gripping too tightly:

Dear Mary,

I joke with my friends that if the world would relinquish all of its power to me, it would be a better place. On some level, and certainly on stressful days, I really believe it. If efficiency and order were all life was about, I would be Queen of the World, at least in my mind. I am not nearly as efficient and orderly as I think I could be if all these people I care about would get out of my way. But that is the rub, isn't it? Life is nothing without the people, and yet it is the people who make it so out of order.

When I am most stressed, and that is pretty frequently these days, I want control. I crave it, demand it, and strive for it. I feel if I could just get things back in control and get a handle on them, then I could prevent the pit in my stomach from coming back. When I am stressed, control seems like the logical answer. As I sit here, I cannot fathom a better one.

My friend Barbara has three children and is the opposite of me when it comes to control. She runs from it. She is laid back and easy. She always says she tries not *to plan too far ahead. She frequently forgets things (like a diaper for her infant on an airplane trip) and just brushes it off. I used to judge her, but now I see that she is clearly happier (at least happy more frequently) than I am, and she feels vibrantly alive. I feel like a slug most of the time. But I just can't; I can't let go of the reins. I feel like it will all fall apart. I feel responsible for running everything in my sphere.*

My husband would have a better life if I were not so control oriented (a.k.a. picky, demanding, aware) because he has a more relaxed approach to life. But when I am in my control mode, I tell myself it is for all of us to have a better life.

Warmly,

Renee

Renee speaks for many women. Wanting control is natural and normal. If we are responsible for everything, it only makes sense that we should be in control. For most of us, getting control represents order, security, and instant gratification. Out of the goodness of our hearts, we sometimes use control as a means to give others what we think they need. We are not controlling in the sense of a control freak or manipulative soap opera vixen. Since going faster didn't work, we're simply developing behaviors to stop us from spinning *out* of control. We have an arsenal of control techniques. We worry more, sleep less, avoid change, strive for perfection, and cry. We feel guilty and sometimes use guilt tactics on others "to keep them safe." We create enormous unrealistic expectations and almost kill ourselves trying to make them a reality. We sometimes try to please at too great a cost or force issues that don't matter.

On bad days, we withhold affection, sex, or money. We stop listening or use the silent treatment. We can be stubborn and refuse to forgive. We don't have to search far to remember the last time we nagged, yelled, or had a meltdown moment. Sometimes we appear unreasonable. I can't be the only woman who has threatened a teenager with a week of no hair spray just so I could feel in control.

But these strategies don't work the way we want them to.

We Try to Control Anyway

Most of us feel it's our duty to get a handle on our health. We eat organic vegetables, drink protein shakes, and kick-box until we ache—and we still get breast and colon cancer and cringe as we watch beautifully fit FloJo, the Olympic gold medalist, die a premature death. We can improve our well-being and increase our odds of living a long life, but we cannot control our mortality.

We put a lot of focus on controlling our jobs. We learn a trade or earn a college degree, collaborate, and "manage our total quality"—and then watch valued colleagues take severance packages. Some of us get a surprise pink slip, often for a job too well or too expensively done. No matter how indispensable we become or how brilliant our ideas, we can't control the business world.

We expect to control our wealth. We save, invest, borrow, and buy mutual funds by the truckloads. We collect credit cards, trade on-line and become dot-com-ers. After riding a roller coaster with the falling yen, diving NASDAQ, soaring college tuition, skyrocketing nursing home bills, and the amicable-turned-bitter divorce that wipes us out, we discover we can't buy control either.

While "vainly" trying to control our appearance we transplant, implant, and "liposuck." We laser, peel, inject, lift, tuck, and dye. Our alterations might make us look a bit better for a little while, but we get old anyway.

We try especially hard to control our children. We choose between breast and bottle, cloth and disposable, private and public. We become experts on the latest research about how and when to toilet train. We worry about quality time, feel guilty about missing the school play, and teach them how to get along in the world. In the end, our children learn to use the bathroom when they are good and ready (and not a minute sooner), become independent and self-reliant, and grow up to be young adults with very distinct ideas of their own on how to live life. We can guide, nurture, and love them, but if we think we can mold them into the people *we* want them to be, we are kidding ourselves.

We commit to our relationships "until death do us part." We learn Victoria's secret, explore who's from Venus and who's from Mars, and look forward to our Golden anniversary—but more than 50 percent of us break up. Despite our focus, getting a handle on love relationships seems extremely elusive.

Our ultimate ambition is to control time. We let Mr. Franklin plan for us, and Ms. Palm pilot our projects. We set goals, write objectives, and devise mission statements. Time may be the stuff life is made of, but we can't stop it, and that makes it impossible to control it.

We spend our talents, energy, and fortunes trying to getting a handle on life, and yet the bottom line is that we really haven't *controlled* diddly-squat.

Don't get me wrong. I am not against low-fat diets, plastic surgery, credit cards, or sexy lingerie. I don't mind electronic devices that remind me how late I am. I'm on record as actually being *in favor of* early toilet training for the last child in the family. I believe in love. These things may contribute to the quality of our lives, but they won't give us control over our lives. And even if they did, trying to control our lives doesn't enrich them. The more we try to control, the poorer we actually become.

Our Pain Is Often Self-Inflicted

Feeling responsible for everything and trying to control all relevant factors can make us physically ill. We already recognize the long list of symptoms attributed to unrelieved stress, from headaches and insomnia to cancer and heart disease. We can't take this knowledge lightly. Jerry Adler in the June 14, 1999, issue of *Newsweek* writes, "Some people make a virtue of stress, under the mantra 'that which does not kill me makes me stronger.' But science shows this to be a lie. A whole new body of research shows the damage stress wreaks on the body: not just heart disease and ulcers, but loss of memory, diminished immune function and even a particular kind of obesity. That which doesn't kill you, it turns out, really does kill you in the end, but first it makes you fat."

The stress from controlling can make me fat? Why didn't someone say so? Now I am listening!

The stress we inflict on ourselves by trying to get a handle on everything takes an emotional toll as well. We become angry, frustrated, overwhelmed, confused, and afraid. Sound familiar? Some might say these emotions put us in danger of losing our souls.

Enough already! you may be thinking. The question is, Why do we strive for control when we know it is physically and emotionally bad for us? The answer: Because we mistake control for strength. We believe in the unspoken conviction that if we are not in control, we are weak and will fail.

The falsehood here is confusing control with a satisfying life.

We also fear that "not in control" or "out of control" means our lives will become a dysfunctional three-ring circus. Who will watch to make sure the trapeze artists don't fall? Our fears are based on faulty notions. Watching the trapeze artists doesn't keep them from falling, and the nervous vigilance prevents us from enjoying the greatest show on earth.

The opposite of control is not chaos.
It is contentment.

We Don't Like to Admit We Control

Perhaps the hairs on the back of your neck are standing up and you are thinking, "How dare she imply I am controlling! What an insult!" If you are feeling uneasy about this idea, you are not alone. We deplore the thought that we might be controlling. It's *so* unfeminine and against our deeply held beliefs about how women should act. Our mothers told us to share, be nice, and take turns. It's important to understand that trying to control doesn't mean we're bad; it means we're coping, perhaps by overusing what comes naturally. We just want to get a handle on things.

I was discussing this topic at a dinner party, and one woman protested, "Well, honestly, I don't think *I* try to control." Her husband looked at her incredulously: "You have to be kidding! Name one thing in your life you don't feel responsible for?" She grinned sheepishly. We can't change what we refuse to recognize. The good news is that if we are willing to make even small adjustments in our thinking and our behavior, we will find a much better way to get what we need to be happier, healthier, and more powerful.

No One Likes It

A great reason to stop using control techniques is that no one likes to be controlled. Do you know anyone who likes it? Do your children, employees, spouse, or friends thank you for trying to be totally in charge of their lives? Striving for control does not endear you to anyone. In fact, it usually gets the opposite reaction. The harder you push, the more they rebel. Again, a law of physics reigns: *For every action, there is an equal and opposite reaction.* In your face or behind your back, you receive a big dose of "you can't make me."

I frequently hear the metaphor "holding the reins too tight," so I asked Wyatt Webb, director of the Equine Experience at the Miraval Spa in Tucson, to explain what happens to a horse when we do that. He said, "When we sit on the horse and squeeze ours legs, we send a signal that says, 'Move forward,' but if we're also pulling back on the reins, we're telling the horse to stop. The contradictory message leaves the horse with no place to go except straight up, and we get bucked off. Failure to give a horse its head means we give it no credit for even knowing how to walk. The animal needs its head for balance, and we cripple it with our urge to be in control. The horse lets us sit on its most vulnerable spot, its spine, and we don't honor that trust by allowing it to participate in a relationship." Wyatt's green eyes peered at me from under the brim of his cowboy hat, and he grinned.

"Our horses weigh well over 1,000 pounds. You're not going to control the animal. The best you can hope for is to solicit its cooperation."

Our subjects may be significantly smaller, but Wyatt's eloquent explanation illustrates why controlling humans doesn't work.

Do We Ever Really Get Control?

One night I said to my discussion group, "We have no control. None. Nada. Zero. Zip." I heard the whole gamut of reactions. One woman retorted swiftly: "Don't insult me! Everyone *knows* you can't control anything. You're not telling me anything I haven't already experienced." For some, you would have thought I had just snatched away Linus's blanket. "You can't tell people that! I can control anything I want to . . . and I can prove it!" Then I was treated to a long rendition of what they could control. I grinned when they said they could control their kids. (I mumbled, "Sure, you can," under my breath.) Others, when asked to write a list of what they could control, jotted something down, stared into space for a minute, then crossed it out, jotted something else, and in a few minutes crossed that out too. One woman yelled, "For crying out loud, Mary, who is going to buy a book that says you can't control anything?" Another lamented, "But, Mary, your ideas are always so positive. What has gotten into you?" (Stick with me. This story has a happy ending.)

Let me make one thing perfectly clear: I am not trying to control *you*. You will have your own ideas about what you can or should ultimately control. The concepts of control or power may mean something entirely different to you. You may *think*—and that is exactly what I want you to do. Powerful women *think*. My goal is not to have you agree with me, but rather to help you examine the role control plays in your life and how it might be interfering with your power. I want to give you specific "works in real-life" solutions to make you an even more powerful woman.

I asked several of my friends to read the manuscript for this book, and one response made me laugh: "Mary, you need to tell the readers up front that you are not a self-righteous, fatalistic zealot so you don't scare them off. Reassure them early on that you're not a nut." Okay. I am not a nut (very often). If I had my druthers I'd start at Chapter Four and launch right into how to be more powerful. But you know how those pesky editors are—always insisting the author reveal what the book is about in the first chapter. It makes sense to begin by exploring what we are doing and why, whether it works, and what a better approach might look like. So, in summary, here are the results of my research on women and control:

- Our language suggests that we want control, and data support that we strive for it, though we view it much differently than men do.

- We feel responsible for just about everything, perhaps in part because our brains are wired that way.

- The vast majority of us are not control freaks; we agree to take the job out of the goodness of our hearts.

- Our strategies don't give us the control we crave, but we pour lots of energy into them anyway, which often results in self-inflicted pain.

- We're deeply insulted when someone implies we're using controlling techniques. Ironically, we use these techniques on others even though we can't think of anyone who likes them.

My analysis of the data? We are fighting a futile battle. So much of our fretting-about, expecting-to, and planning-on energy is wasted. Yearning for control doesn't give us the freedom, peace, and connection we all want. It doesn't satisfy the sense of security and order we crave. It makes us physically ill, mentally exhausted, and spiritually drained.

Striving for control doesn't work very well or very often. It does not make us powerful.

The Alternative

You may be asking yourself, "If I am supposed to stop striving for control, what is the alternative?" I remember a discussion I had with a psychiatrist friend. She had a patient addicted to cocaine and struggling to recover. My friend said the most difficult aspect of getting a patient to give up her addiction is finding a substitute that makes her feel as good. In this book, you will learn about six powers you can use to counter the urge to control and substitute strategies that will make you feel not just good but even better.

But I Am Afraid—and Skeptical

I was too. If I thought having control was feasible, believe me, as the original Queen Bee of Control herself, I would write a book on how to get more of it. Hard as it is, we must accept the fact that striving for control is not only counterproductive, draining, and a waste of time; being in control all the time is impossible. Sustaining it ranks right up there with Santa Claus, the tooth fairy, and the pot of gold at the end of the rainbow. It would be nice if those things were real, but they're not. The good news is that striving for control is a bad habit you can break. I realize that relinquishing control may seem like a foreign concept right now, maybe even a really bad idea. Perhaps you're busy making a list of things in your head that you *can* control. Habits die hard.

If you have read the Contents page, and the chapters titled "Slow Up," "Wise Up," and "Pair Up" make you want to Throw Up, take heart. This book is a leap of faith. You'll have doubts and maybe even experience fierce resistance. You might make some progress and then relapse. Some concepts may be initially hard to buy into. Go easy. If you keep an open mind, I promise not to ask you to give up anything that is worth keeping. Together we will walk through the process.

If your mind is racing and you are wondering what these six powers are and how they work and why I don't just tell you now, may I politely say, "Hey! Stop trying to control my chapter!" You have my word that we'll get to all that. In the following chapters, you will learn about how you can move from striving for control to thriving with power.

Some months ago Dr. Joyce Brothers wrote in *Parade* magazine, "We didn't design the seas, so we can't control the currents; and we didn't design the boat, so we can't make it impregnable, but we can steer to our own satisfaction, and let go of the rest. Looking at it that way, maybe the job we have to do isn't so overwhelming."

Indeed!

POWER UP
Tapping into Energy

So what makes us feel better than trying to get a handle on everything? The spiritual gurus tell us that we need to let go. That's probably sage advice, but I have been holding on for dear life, and maybe like you, I am afraid to let go. I envision falling into a big black abyss full of dirty laundry, unpaid bills, and missed appointments. I confess that sweet surrender never sounded all that sweet to me.

Feeling in control gives us a temporary sense of instant gratification. We operate under the equation:

Control = Feeling good about ourselves.

It naturally follows that if a little control could make us feel good, wouldn't a lot of control make us blissful? We rely on this possibility because we don't know what else to do.

We've been clutching this formula, sensing it doesn't work, but we have lacked a viable alternative. This chapter is about finding a new equation for feeling good about ourselves.

Back to the Basics

The next logical question we need to ask is, If control is so hard to come by, are we simply billions of amoeba-like creatures aimlessly bumping into each other in a big vat of blueberry and lime-green gelatin? Of course not. Our own experiences confirm that although we can't guarantee outcomes, we have enormous power to become a change agent. The operative word here is *power*. *Webster's* defines power as "having a great ability to do, act or affect strongly. Vigor. Strength." Notice it does not include any of the definitions of *control:* "To exercise authority over, to hold back, to curb," and, as a noun, "the condition of being restrained."

There's an alternative to striving for control to get what we want. The new equation is based on the Principle of Energy Flow, the Principle of Timing, and the Principle of Trust.

PRINCIPLE OF ENERGY FLOW

When we attempt to get what we want by controlling, we use force. We *wage a war* on poverty or on drugs. We *push* ourselves until we *suffer combat* fatigue. We *fight* the *battle* of the bulge. Controlling the problem becomes our sole focus. But here's the irony:

We don't ultimately want control.
Control is the means, not the end.

What we want is *energy.* Energy is what life is all about: energy to get things done, to keep the peace, to enjoy relationships, to express ourselves creatively, to gain cooperation, to make a difference, and to love. We need energy to keep up. But we deplete our energy reserves striving to obtain a sense of control. Think about it. Being responsible for everything is exhausting! We waste so much energy that we feel weak, fearful, and wanting at the end of the day.

So how do we move from the illusion of control to the reality of energy? Letting go is the answer, but not in the sense you might think. Let's reexamine the concept of letting go.

GIVE AND TAKE AND EBB AND FLOW

Think of "controlling" as holding your breath. You can do it for a while, and it will seem as if you're in charge: You're definitely not going to let the air come out! But then something more powerful than your will to control takes over—

in this case, carbon dioxide levels in your blood signal your brain to pass out—so you exhale and begin to breath.

When people are emotionally "out of control," we often suggest they slow down and breathe deeply. "Come on," we coax. "Sit down a minute, and take a few deep breaths." We never say, " You are so upset. Let's see how long you can hold your breath." We associate energy, peace, and calmness with breathing deeply.

Yet you can't take a new breath if you don't let go of the old one. Exhaling—*letting go* of the air—is the *power* move. Athletes know this. When they lift weights in the gym, they lift the bar off their chest into the air as they exhale. They blow out and let that energy make them stronger. Letting go does not mean you become spineless, dependent, apathetic, or incapable. It means you tap into your energy. You do not waste it forcing, judging, limiting, or withholding. This allows energy to flow to and through you, and you get more of what you want.

THE POWER OF LETTING GO

Fortunately, this energy is readily available. We don't need more money, long-term therapy, or a faster Internet connection. We simply need an intense desire to stop squeezing so tightly, making sure everything turns out all right, and ending up exhausted from holding on, going nowhere. If you let go, you can use your powers to get you into the flow of life.

My friend Kym Croft Miller, lawyer-turned-children's-author and mother of three little girls, was struggling with the final stanza of her new children's book based on Shakespearean plays. The lines "came to her" when she "took a breather" and spent the day at the Oregon beach with her kids. She called to read me the stanza and tell me about her experience with the power of letting go:

> *The time is now*
> *To join the fun*
> *No matter what your age.*
> *The play is yours*
> *Because you see*
> *All the world's a stage.*

Then she sent me this e-mail:

> *Just a quick note because I was thinking of our conversation this morning. It hit me that the great thing about having the inspiration come to me at the beach was not only that, as you mentioned, it probably would not have come if I had scheduled it (e.g., "9:00 A.M.–9:30—have powerful creative insight") but it was the unexpectedness that carried a lot of the juice. I was practically high the whole day just because some-*

*thing had come out of the blue in a totally unplanned place. It
was thrilling. What was also funny was that I had not planned
to write at the beach. I always carry some paper with me but
failed to bring a pen. When we put our stuff down by this beautiful old log, I noticed a pen in the sand, and when the thoughts
came to me, I just started writing them down. I really feel at
those moments that the universe, God, whatever one believes
in, rewards us for our act of trust, our letting go of the reins.
When I am too structured, that is what I miss out on—the profound and amazing energy that is our reward.*

Kym's experience illustrates perfectly how the first principle works:

Energy is our reward for letting go.

Time and again, when you overcome your urge to control, energy will be the payoff. It doesn't matter what you are
writing: your grocery list, the proposal for a new client, or
your life goals. Relaxing and opening up to possibilities allows energy to flow through you. A natural high truly is the
reward.

So now you may be thinking, "Okay, swell. I'm all for
more energy and natural highs. This stuff sounds good in
yoga journals, but how do I make this work in real life?" The
second principle is your key.

PRINCIPLE OF TIMING

Control *demands*. It's the epitome of impatience. Control insists on its own timetable. But insights, inspiration, and answers have a schedule independent of our protests. The greatest lessons of all were found while standing on the tops of mountains, sitting under trees, and during forty days of isolation in the desert. The most powerful humans who ever lived *waited*. Gandhi didn't start shouting, "Okay, let's get this show on the road. I don't have much time here!"

Letting go *invites*. It creates the circumstances for opportunity to visit. Control creates expectations. Letting go embraces surprise and mystery.

We want to be women who can make things happen. But often our meddling and our impatience give us the opposite of what we are striving for. In his book *Callings: Finding and Following an Authentic Life,* Gregg Levoy tells a story of a man "helping" a butterfly emerge from his cocoon. But the butterfly died; without the drying process of breaking out, his wings were too wet to survive. Levoy wrote, "We do much damage by not being patient with our own evolution, which by design and necessity luxuriates in an abundance of time and plot twists. We communicate to our souls that we do not have faith in them, in their intimacy with the creative force of life. We sneak downstairs in the middle of the night to see if the elves are sewing things up. We force the fauna with our hot insistent breath. We rush a verdict so we can get home in time for dinner. We try to make things happen, hoping that in doing so we don't inadvertently open the darkroom, behind which fate is developing our pictures."

Letting go is the missing link in this process. Drumming our fingers, tapping our feet, and making our mental lists won't make things go faster or give us control over how our lives will unfold. It's all too easy to squander our energy by demanding that our timing must drive the world. Timing *is* everything, and letting go requires patience.

Are you wondering, " Gee, if I don't have much control, then who does?" The answer lies in the third principle of letting go.

PRINCIPLE OF TRUST

Fear always precipitates our impulse to control, and the only known antidote to fear is faith. Relinquishing control requires putting our trust in something or someone. We place our faith in a variety of places. Some women believe that God has a plan for each of us, and others contend that everything happens for a reason. Do you presume that some things are just meant to be and you place your confidence in fate, destiny, or karma? My British friend Patricia Dick told me about being quite frightened when she was trapped in a London subway during a bomb scare. Her companion, nonplussed, simply said, "There's no reason to be afraid. If your number's up, it's up."

In listening to the various opinions, I found a kind of faith continuum, with a total commitment to predestiny and "the devil made me do it" on one end and chaos theory, where even randomness has an order, on the other. I found little signs in my own office that suggested that I too thought there was a method to the madness. On my bulletin board I have a poster that reads:

Everything in the universe is subject to change and everything is on schedule.

I received the following letter from Annette Simmons, president of Group Process Consulting. She beautifully portrays for us how her faith is a prerequisite to letting go of control and using her power:

Dear Mary,

When I started my business, I knew exactly how I wanted things to turn out. I had done all the visualizations, written a detailed business plan, and chosen a business partner. I spent money on brochures outlining the workshops I would teach and the services I would offer. God, however, had other ideas. They say if you want to make God laugh, just make a plan. He would've been rolling at the details I had conjured up.

Anyway, after the first month, we had not achieved the detailed goals I had outlined. I got more detailed and broke the goals down into weekly objectives. Then one month later, my partner quit. It was a terrible shock. He hadn't realized the work involved becoming an entrepreneur, his wife wanted a paycheck, and the fact that I kept checking up on him probably didn't help. Nevertheless, I rebounded and revised my plan so I could feel in control again. One week later, I was hit by a truck (literally!) My car was totaled, and my brain was fuzzy. By that time, I felt that every time I stood up and regained my hold of the controls, something kept knocking me back down into the dirt. I dusted myself off one more time, and one more time I was knocked down when a client delayed a job I was counting on until next year. By then, it was late November 1997. This time I just sat there in the dirt. I was tired of getting back up again. I decided to boycott the rest of 1997. Up to that point, it had turned out so badly I reasoned that sitting out for the month of December couldn't do any more harm.

Fortunately the real result of my boycotting the rest of the year was that I let go of the controls. I stopped trying to force things to happen. I found myself observing and listening more and talking and planning less. I gave up trying to make things happen and began to tune into what was already happening. I wrote a proposal for a new book that had nothing to do with my goals and objectives and had everything to do with what I found useful and interesting to me. I called and talked to people without an agenda, just to connect. This is when my fortunes turned around. I now have more business than I can handle,

> *my new book comes out in May, and none of it came from*
> *"planning your work and working your plan." It came from*
> *backing off, listening, and letting God lead. I think that no*
> *matter how good a dancer I may think I am, I end up looking a*
> *lot better on the dance floor when I let someone who knows*
> *what He is doing lead.*
>
> *Warmly,*
>
>
> *Annette*

Whether you believe in God, fate, or mood rings, letting go requires trust.

The New Equation

If you are willing to open up to the possibilities, be patient with the evolution of events, and have faith in some force other than yourself, you are ready for the new equation. Keep in mind that what we're after is energy. As I developed my thoughts on this, I wrote to my friend Melanie Mills, a speaker and author, and she replied,

> *So your idea of power is really about energy . . . energy to*
> *move you forward in a direction that is constructive and fulfill-*

ing. There is a moment of surrender if the results I am getting
are not what I want and I look again for a choice or an attitude
that might serve me better. Hmmmm, the wheels are turning.

I hope yours are too.

An old saying advises, "Do everything in your power
and then let go." I believe a better approach is:

Let go, and then do everything with your power.

So it's time for new terminology:

**Powering up: Letting go of control and allowing energy
to flow.**

By powering up, we take control out of the formula. Instead of, "Control = Feeling good about yourself," the new
equation now reads:

Powering up = Feeling good about yourself.

Imagine the old equation as a kinked hose. The energy
is there. It wants to flow through, but something is squeezing the hose too tight and the blockage causes pressure
(stress, illness) to build. The new equation releases the kink
and allows the energy to flow and move freely.

I received a letter from the mother of an eight year old who illustrates how this works:

Dear Mary,

> *I remember feeling so strongly that I had to protect my first daughter from people who didn't approach life the way I did. For example, her grandmother is an amazingly warm and loving person, but she requires politeness to a much greater degree than I do. For quite a while, I would try to be a go-between with them, telling Jenna to say* please *or explaining or apologizing to her grandma. Then one visit it struck me. Wasn't my job to let Jenna experience different people and then help her to work through her own feelings about them and discover why they do what they do? I was doing such a disservice with my control of the situations and exchanges she had, not to mention how stressful it was for me. Now I let her have her own independent relationship with her grandmother, which is much better without me in the middle. When she is confused, we talk about it (e.g., "Well, why do you think Grandma didn't respond well when you said that?" or "Why do you think her feelings were hurt when you did that?") No blame. No judgment. No control. We just explore it together. It feels like an amazing burden has been lifted from all of us.*

This mother used the new equation so effectively. She let go of her need to be responsible for all the relationships in her family, and she patiently waited for her daughter to discover her own lessons. She had faith that she alone did not have to be in charge. Notice the last line of her letter: "It feels like an amazing burden has been lifted *from all of us.*" Energy was everyone's reward for powering up.

We Teach What We Most Need to Learn

Writing the first chapter of this book was a case study itself in learning how to power up and use the new equation. *I tried with all my might to control a book about control.* And every time I did, I stalled. Only when I tapped into the powers that I write about in this book did I get insights, make progress, and enjoy the ride. Only then did I feel good about myself.

I really procrastinated writing the first chapter. I arrived home after a long trip, and I yearned to pet the cat, weed the garden, and clean the house. I had lived out of a suitcase for seven weeks, and I wanted some beauty and order. I also knew, however, that I had a deadline to meet. Despite my considerable jet lag, I set an ambitious goal to write on my first day back. But my right brain pleaded, "Couldn't we please just clean up the office first? It's such a mess, and it would feel so nice to write in a neat space. Haven't you ever heard of feng shui? Clutter blocks our chi." I bristled. "You're just stalling, and no one is going to write this chapter for us, so let's not waste time."

My brain would not give in. "Ah, come on. Let's just organize that big stack of old books." I was annoyed at myself for not being more disciplined, but I relented. "Okay, but just this one stack."

As I was sorting the pile, I came across a book called *Illusions* by Jonathan Bach. "How ironic to find this," I thought. I had received a letter several days previously from a client telling me *Illusions* was her favorite book and I should add it to the recommended book list on my Web site. I read the first few pages. I had forgotten how much I liked it and lay down on the sofa to read just a little bit more. My eyes grew heavy, and before I knew it, I woke up from a two-hour nap. Groggy and in a dim light, I grabbed my notebook, and the outline for the entire chapter poured out, detailed and in precise order. In a delicious flash of synchronicity, my pen explained to me the *illusion* of control.

I had the power to write the chapter. Somehow my brain knew how to tap into that energy by letting go long enough to listen to my inner voice, read some beautiful words, and renew myself with sleep. You have this power too. You have tremendous untapped energy ready to flow to you, available just for the asking.

Still Balking?

Making changes takes practice. At first the concept of letting go was about as attractive to me as having little black hairs grow on my chin. I'm convinced powering up is one of the answers to our problem of having too much to do. Give power a chance.

A passage in *The Little Book of Letting Go* by Hugh Prather inspired me: "Some things are simple, and here's one of them: You can relax and let go of your life, in which case you will know peace. Or you can try to control your life, in which case you will know war." Perhaps you're thinking, "But exactly how do I do that? I'd find it easier to buy into the concept of powering up if I knew some specific strategies. With the world moving so fast and responsibility weighing so heavily on my shoulders, how on earth do I let go so that this so-called energy will flow through me?"

So glad you asked. In the next chapter, you will learn how to use the concept of microactions to help you begin tapping into more of your power.

BREAK IT UP
Using Microactions

I F WE WANT to power up, we'll need to make some changes, and most of us are already up to our armpits in change. How could more change possibly help? Say the C word, and an invisible barrier pops up that often prevents us from doing what we really want to do. Microactions ease our resistance.

I introduced the concept of microactions in my book *Stop Screaming at the Microwave! How to Connect Your Disconnected Life.* Microactions are teeny-tiny steps that propel us forward without threatening our sense of control. They get around our fears because we commit to something so little we could hardly be afraid, and we're guaranteed success. They're much smaller than steps and often so ridiculous that we outfox our resistance to change.

I first learned about the power of microactions when I

used the concept to help my patients make dramatic alterations in their lifestyles. As the director of the Hypertension Research Center at the University of Colorado Health Sciences Center, I prescribed exercise for all my patients who wanted to lose weight. I remember one woman who hated to exercise. I honestly think she would rather wire her jaw shut, staple her stomach, or eat a strict diet of earthworms. At each visit, I instructed her to walk for thirty minutes three times a week, and at each return visit she confessed she had not exercised at all. We tried every behavior modification trick in the book, but no amount of punishment or reward would get her to comply.

So I tried a microaction. I asked her if she could simply get dressed to exercise three times a week. She looked at me as if I was radioactive. "What a worthless thing to do! Let me get this straight. I am suppose to just *get dressed* to exercise? A sweatshirt will not burn any calories!"

I agreed but replied, "Just this week. Humor me. Please."

At her next visit, I asked her if she had tried the "just get dressed" prescription.

"Yes, I did."

"Great! Now I want you to add one minute of walking . . ."

She interrupted me with an crafty grin. "I walked for thirty minutes three times this week."

"But I gave you strict instructions not to."

She laughed. "I felt so stupid standing there, all dressed up with no place to go, that I decided to walk just a little. Five blocks from home, I discovered that exercise isn't so bad. My neighbor has joined me, so between the hiking and the verbal venting, I come back feeling wonderful."

I Bet You Have a Pair, Too

Jaye Lunsford read about using microactions to lose weight in *Stop Screaming at the Microwave!* and applied the principle with great success. She wrote, "I now fit into my 'hope jeans.' They're the ones every woman has in a drawer somewhere. She hasn't fit into them since college, but someday she hopes they will fit again. These jeans are literally older than some of my colleagues. What a treat!"

How did she do it? Instead of approaching weight loss as most of us do—trying to control the weight with guilt, punishment, and deprivation—Jaye used microactions to fit into those hope jeans by telling herself, "No, Jaye, you do not have to *do* the exercise video yet. You don't even have to *watch* it yet. Just start by putting the box on top of the VCR. Okay?" After looking at the box every day, she finally popped the tape in, took a few steps, and discovered she liked to exercise at home. Her hope jeans fit like a dream.

Oh, Pleeeease. Get Real.

Do microactions seem too small to have a real impact? You may be surprised to learn that research shows little things can make a profound difference in our lives. Dr. Norbert Schwartz, a psychologist at the University of Michigan's Institute for Social Research, states that our moods often determine our overall satisfaction with our lives. Quoted in the *St. Louis Dispatch,* he says, "Very minimal things can put you temporarily in a good mood" and thus brighten everything else. In one study, a dime was occasionally placed on a photocopier for the next user to find. Later, everyone who had used the machine was interviewed. "Those who found the dime were happier and more satisfied and wanted to change their lives less than those who didn't find the dime," explained Schwartz. Another study asked people leaving a grocery store to evaluate their satisfaction with their TVs at home. Those who minutes earlier got a free food sample from the store liked their TVs better than those who missed the sample.

A dime makes us love life, and a free food sample makes us happier with our TVs? And you wondered if wacky microactions really work. Don't worry about being able to power up. We're surprisingly easy to outsmart. Think of the least threatening action, and give it a whirl. Do you want to clean out the closet but have trouble letting go of your perfectionism? Move one hanger a day. By the week's end, you will actually see some progress, and maybe you will block off an hour to finish it. I have found that the tinier and seemingly less useful the action is, the more it works in getting past our resistance to change. Attempt something really ludicrous. Want more time to read? Set your alarm for one minute earlier. What will one minute of reading do? Nothing. That's the idea. How can you resist something that makes no difference? It could, however, have a big impact if you keep setting it one minute each night.

Why do microactions work? Linda Sapadien, author of *Beat Procrastination and Master the Grade,* says, "Microactions help us overcome our 'yes, but factor' by getting us into a flow of energy. We stick our toe in the river and we get caught up in the energy flow of that small action, a current that takes us to completion." She added that they help us "tap into our powers because microactions move us from the mental wish, *I want to do this,* to the action, *I can do this.*"

Serious Stuff

Some of you might be thinking, "I have complicated, longstanding, and practically impossible-to-solve problems. Will microactions help me let go of control when it comes to the big issues in life?"

Don't confuse the seeming silliness of the step with the effectiveness of the effort. Wendy Baker attended my seminar and then wrote to me that she was "rushing along at breakneck speed and was detoured by a masterful roadblock, anorexia nervosa." She described her affliction, perhaps one of the best examples of what our desire for control can do to our bodies and our lives, as "a lying, sneaking, deceiving, and cheating disease."

Dear Mary,

I see a nutritionist regularly to formulate a diet to help me safely put the weight back on that I lost. Part of my meal plan consists of eating a carton of yogurt and an apple every night after a complete dinner, no matter what. I know, I know, it sounds easy, or even healthy to most of you, but remember, I still have this devil called anorexia living inside me that twists and converts all logical thoughts in my mind. I start adding up the calories that are going into my body with each bite, the calories that are putting me back on the road to health and safety, and I see killing poisons that I am deliberately injecting into myself. When I began this part of the meal plan, I would physically shake so hard that I could barely get a spoon up to my mouth. Tears streamed down my face, and anger flashed

through my soul. I was in a constant battle with myself, logic
versus anorexia—and anorexia was obviously winning.

The turning point in her private war came when she tried a microaction. Her mother, seeing her struggle to control her eating night after night, brought out Mancala, an African game of strategy played by dropping polished stones into bins on a wooden board. Two players compete to get the most stones in their bin by the time the first player runs out. After every dinner, the two women amused themselves with the stones until Wendy finished eating the apple and yogurt. She wrote, "Slowly, my focus turned from my food to the game. Mancala is literally saving my life."

How was it saving her life? The game was more than a mere distraction. For Wendy, motion was the enemy. She wanted to bolt from the table when she saw the additional food. She had to find a way to sit still so she could complete the agonizing task of eating an apple and a carton of yogurt. Saying she would just sit down and eat a slice of apple or a spoonful of yogurt was too big a step, filling her with terror and causing her to shake and cry. Her microaction was aimed at helping her stay at the table long enough to overcome her anxieties. Remember that fear is always behind our urge to control. Wendy reminds us of a microaction's potency, even an indirect one, to help us overcome our panic. If a teeny-tiny strategy can help her power up against her irrational desire to starve, I bet the concept could work for you too. (In the spirit of "everybody loves a happy ending," I spoke with Wendy three years after she initially wrote to me. She is totally recovered, just got married, and couldn't be happier.)

Gonna Do to Follow Through

With every idea I offer you, I look for ways to test the concepts in my own life. I love to write, but I procrastinated nearly every day writing this book. Each morning I'd start to control and obsess: "What if I can't think of anything? What if it isn't good enough? And how will I get all my other work done if I write all morning?" I could see the stall tactics begin. I watered plants. I sorted mail. I felt a deep need to disinfect the kitchen counters. So I'd walk over to the computer and turn it on. After all, I would need a working computer. Then I'd think about calling my cousin, fixing my chipped nail, and thawing something for dinner. I'd become overwhelmed with an intense desire to finally finish my fifteen-year-old son's baby album. Then I'd patiently tell myself, "You do not have to write a book. You just have to type the word *the*." I'd type it in. *The* looked pretty stupid on the screen, so I'd write, "Do you try to control things by procrastinating? So do I." Aha! The beginning of a paragraph. Two little microactions, and I was writing!

Let's face it: Sometimes we're reluctant to give up control because we worry that someone else will take over and *probably do it all wrong.* One mother confessed this was her barrier to letting go. She came home from work late and discovered her two little boys running around in just their briefs. When she quizzed her husband about why they weren't wearing pajamas, he said, "Oh, I bathed them, but I knew that no matter what I gave them to wear, you would change their clothes when you got home. So I just decided to wait." At that moment, she knew she'd better try a few easy microactions before she started on the big decisions. "So I practiced by letting go of my desire to make sure my sons wore the perfect PJs. I know it sounds lame, but that little step helped me see a lot of other areas that I was needlessly controlling."

Maybe you too are reticent to let go of the big stuff. Don't despair. Try a few microactions on minor decisions, and ease your way in. It will help you let go of control and move yourself from "gonna do" to "follow through."

Ready, Set, GO!

We're at the end of Part One. We have laid the ground-work to help us power up: to let go so that energy will flow through us. We know that control is an illusion and that striving for it will make us exhausted, sick, and crazy, if it hasn't already. Energy will be our reward if we're willing to thwart our urge to have a handle on everything. With patience and faith, we can take little microactions toward using a new equation of feeling good.

You're now ready to tap into the six powers. I have

arranged this book to make it very easy for you to explore the concepts of control and power in your own life. Each chapter of Part Two highlights a specific power. These chapters contain Things to Think About: stories and examples that encourage you to examine your own power from many different points of view. You'll find practical and innovative strategies that will teach you how to move from striving for control to thriving with power. These strategies are summed up toward the end of the chapter in the Tools for Your Repair Kit section—so named because if your handle on life is broken, you need the tools to repair it.

Sprinkled throughout the chapters are microactions—the teeny-tiny steps to propel you past your resistance to let go. And you will also learn how to use your ABCs of Power—the power to Act, the power to Believe, and the power to Choose—to live a peaceful and purposeful life.

Each chapter then ends with an especially inspiring letter or e-mail sent to me illustrating a valuable lesson about powering up and a final message that I call a Hot Flash of Power. The author Joan Borysenko refers to hot flashes as "power surges of wisdom and strength." Therefore, this final message is a summary statement to remind you to let go and then do everything with your power.

You are a powerful woman! Turn the page, and let's continue the journey.

TWO

The Six Powers in Your Repair Kit

SLOW UP
Pause Before Judging

M Y HUSBAND RETURNED home one day from our (then) ten-year-old son's wrestling practice. Joe stood in the kitchen moping like a kid bringing home a bad report card. I asked, "What's wrong?"

He sighed. "Well, I was standing against the gym wall watching the boys wrestle. The coach is not very organized, and he was trying to teach the boys ten different moves in one session. There were mats and little kids everywhere, arms and legs flailing, with the coach shouting over the din. One of the mothers comes every week and films the entire session. I stood there in the middle of this chaos, thinking how overbearing she was to videotape every weekly practice. She was so focused on filming that she ran into me. I tried not to react, but she must have sensed my disapproval.

She turned to me and said, 'I'm so sorry for bumping you.' Then, as an afterthought, she pointed to her son and said, 'You know, it's just the two of us. Of course, I know nothing about wrestling, and the coach goes over a dozen different instructions. So I leave work a little early on practice days so I can film the moves. Then we go back to our apartment, and I try to help my son so he doesn't get behind. He just loves wrestling.' "

I smiled at my kind-hearted husband. "So you feel lower than a snake's belly for judging her? If there was a scumbag parade, you could be the grand marshal?"

He grimaced. "You have no idea how bad I feel."

Many of us might have viewed the situation just as Joe did: The woman must be an overly protective mother who still cuts the kid's meat at dinner, and *that* is why she's filming every week. We're all susceptible to filling in the blanks—even a really nice person like my husband. But when we do, more often than not, we fill it in all wrong, and we end up feeling rotten. Besides being unfair, this approach drains our energy and does not give us the control we're seeking.

When we don't have all the facts, we feel out of control. It's hard to make a logical decision with incomplete data. This absence of detailed information creates anxiety. What do we do to gain back our sense of control? We make stuff up and fill in the blanks. We see a small part of what is going on and rush to judgment. We rationalize that our added "information" is obvious, common sense, or the most likely explanation. Many of us do this so often and so efficiently we don't even realize it's our feeble attempt to control the unknown.

It Comes Easily

Our inborn feminine talents encourage us to "be in the know." Research reveals that women are innately predisposed to apply more intuitive and imaginative judgments to situations than men do. We excel at picking up on tiny inflections of voice or changes in facial expressions and body postures. We don't necessarily need cold, hard, and overt facts to know the "truth."

We also like to share what we know. Women love to gossip, "because," as Helen Fischer writes in *The First Sex,* "this intimate word-filled pastime connects them to their confidantes, making and sustaining ties that women see as power."

But sometimes gossiping includes filling in a few blanks, and when we act on those erroneous assumptions, we diminish our power. In *The Four Agreements,* Don Miguel Ruiz writes, "The whole world of control between humans is about making assumptions. . . . Our whole dream of hell is based on that." We create emotional poisons—sadness, drama, loss, guilt, fear, envy, anger—when we try to control our uncontrollable world by filling in the blanks too quickly.

The good news is that we can gain power if we learn to pause before judging. It's amazingly easy, especially if we start with microactions. We don't necessarily need to enlist the cooperation of others. It doesn't take more time, require new training, or cost a cent. Everything that we need to use this power is already inside us. Best yet, pausing counteracts our compulsion to leap to often incorrect conclusions.

Here are Things to Think About to help you use the power of the pause.

I Know What You Must Be Thinking

One of my clients told me about the time she and her husband went to a restaurant with their twenty -month-old child. She said, "We knew better than to try to go out to dinner with a toddler this age, but we were desperate for a change of scenery. Adam acted just like twenty month olds do at restaurants—throwing food, laughing, jumping around, and making a big mess. When we go out to dinner, the cost of the actual meal is cheap. What *is* expensive is the tip we have to leave the waitress for running the industrial-sized Shop-Vac after we leave. An older couple at a nearby table kept looking at us, watching Adam's every move. We knew their meal was ruined because of our commotion. We were so uncomfortable with their stares that we left before our meal was over. As we walked by their table, the woman spoke up: 'We hope you didn't mind that we watched your precious little boy. Our grandson is just about that age. We haven't seen him in over a year, and we know that he's probably doing the same things as your little one. It was such a pleasure to see how happy your son is!' "

My client laughed, "Mary, you are absolutely right. I was filling in the blanks, and I was filling them in all wrong. I could have kicked myself for ruining our meal out."

We might be good people-readers, but most of us are lousy mind readers. When we hastily fill in the blanks we're often way off the mark.

"Don't borrow trouble," my mother used to say. For the next week, try a simple microaction. Ask yourself with each emotional upset you experience: Do I have all the facts, or have I presupposed some of the details? Would it help to pause, back up, and get the real scoop?

It's a Me Me Me World

I received this letter from Diane Mathews:

Dear Mary,

I attended your workshop and found the hardest assignment you gave was to discuss times when we had filled in the blanks of a situation, ending up with a completely different interpretation from what was real or intended.

When I heard the assignment, I agreed immediately that it happens often, but I was hard-pressed to think of an actual situation where it had happened to me. I could have described multiple times it had been played out on TV sit-coms or in a Dear Abby column. But come up with a personal experience? I was stymied.

It finally dawned on me why: Because I do not take the time (chance?) to check with people to find out why they said or did what they did. I'm living in the World According to Me. If that is how I interpret a situation, then it MUST be true! And my guess is, I am not the only one who lives in this world.

I'll allow that there are times when we don't do a fact check because we do not want to find out that someone thinks we are at fault, or an idiot, or did something imperfectly. We'd rather just fill in the blanks in a way that plays us in a rosy light.

Sometimes we don't do a fact check because we have al-

ready taken action that is based on our perception of what has happened. If we find out the real facts, we may have to redo our actions.

Sometimes we don't do a fact check because it simply doesn't matter to us one way or another. So my first microaction is to be aware of times I am filling in blanks. My second is to analyze why I am doing it, and if doing a reality check is appropriate, I can do it. At least I'll be able to avoid taking action that has to be retooled once I get the whole story.

Diane describes many of us. We don't do a fact check because we're not sure we'll like reality as well as we like our personally invented version of the situation. We tend to see what we want to see and hear what we want to hear. Some days we live by the truism, "Ignorance is bliss." We also don't do a fact check because we've made our plans based on our assumptions, and if we find out we assumed wrong, the new truth could really wreak havoc. Finally, many of us are simply indifferent. We rationalize, "What possible significance could such a little detail have?" Many of us are so fixated on controlling *our* world that we take most events and put them through the filter of "how this affects *me.*"

I learned Diane's lesson the hard way one day. I flew to a small town on the East Coast last year, which meant I had to change from a nice big 747 to one of those Tonka Toy planes where everyone has both a window *and* an aisle seat. Our small group of travelers trudged out onto the tarmac, anxious to get on board. An airline official decided that a woman in a wheelchair should board first. She took one step onto the stairs, and suddenly it began to rain. Within minutes, the wind whipped up, impaling icy drops into our faces. We stood there in the downpour, watching her slowing ascend the stairs.

Two steps from the top, she collapsed to her knees, and try as she might, she could not pull herself up. The handful of us at the bottom of the stairs had two reactions: One group could not take their eyes off her as she knelt stranded in midair. Eyes bored into this woman, willing her to stand up. The other group diverted their eyes, tried to cover their sopping wet heads with their briefcases, and looked down at the puddles.

The flight attendant stood at the door of the plane, trying unsuccessfully to lift the woman. He motioned for help. A baggage handler ran up the steps and tried to lift from behind. I sympathized with the woman's plight and silently prayed for her, but after a while, I stood there thinking of the absurdity of this situation. I looked as if I'd survived a tsunami and could only envision the first impression I would make when my client picked me up at the next airport—assuming I would ever arrive at my destination. I could feel my canvas carry-on bag getting heavier and knew the papers inside were getting wetter by the minute. I also knew the clothes in my luggage (which was sitting on the tarmac waiting for the baggage handler to get the woman on board) were probably soaked too. I pictured in my mind a ruined pale pink suit.

Out of the cold mist, a man behind me who was looking up at the woman still struggling to move said, "Now there's a lady who must *really* want to go somewhere!"

Oh, my. I immediately realized that I was in the World According to Me. *I* was wet. *I* was tired. *I* was impatient. But *I* wasn't stuck at the top of a stairway in the middle of a rainy airfield with a dozen travelers staring at me. I could walk up a flight of stairs. I would dry out. I could buy a new suit. I had filled in the vacuum with how this event affected *me*. In my mind I was chattering, "Can't someone else load this luggage? Have they ever heard of umbrellas? If they had used a jetway, this wouldn't be happening. Why did my travel agent put me on such a dinky plane?" My controlling mind-set was making me miserable. Me, me, me! I felt so ashamed of myself! If only I had used my power to pause before judging. As a result of just one little remark, the attitude of the whole crowd changed, and we endured the downpour with a little more grace and gratitude after this kind and insightful man put us in our place.

A few of my colleagues discouraged me from telling this story: "Gee, Mary, you sound so self-centered and unkind, and you're not." I appreciate their vote of confidence, and I'd love to tell you that I never have a less than charitable thought, that I fill in the blanks only with other people's best interests in mind. Wouldn't we all like to think of ourselves as people who spend most of our time taking homemade casseroles to shut-ins? The brutal truth is that sometimes I reside in the World According to Me, and I can tell you that it's a dreary, lonely place. Whenever I find myself there, I now take a microaction by asking, "Is there another way to fill in this blank?"

We create many of our own problems in a one-woman world. Look around, listen up, let go, and let others into your life. As you gain another's perspective, your urge to control will begin to melt away.

Prince Charming Rides Away

My good friend Jane met the man of her dreams when she was thirty-three, and in a matter of weeks, they talked in detail about getting married. Then one day he told her that although he did not have any real doubts about his love for her, he wanted time to consider his intentions. Just a few months before, he had left a very short, rather disastrous marriage, and he wanted to examine his fears of jumping into a lifelong commitment again. He felt he needed some time to think.

Jane called me in tears.

I asked her, "Has he stopped calling you?"

"No."

"Has he stopped seeing you?"

"No."

"Is he just as close and affectionate? Does he still seem to enjoy your company?"

"Very much so. We are as close as ever. But he said he needs time to think things through. He wants to resolve a few issues within himself before he makes a commitment. I'm sure he is going to leave me, so I am going to make the first move."

"Whoa, Jane, hold on a minute. Stop filling in the blanks and worrying about something that may not even happen. You're trying to control whether you get hurt. But it doesn't really matter who says good-bye. You are in love with him. If you break up, you'll get hurt. Besides, there is no evidence to suggest he's *leaving*. He's *just thinking*. This is a test. Only a test. If this were a true emergency, he would be backing off and making excuses of why he can't be with you. Trust takes time to earn. He just got badly burned. He would have to have a very low IQ to think that diving back in so quickly, without any soul searching, is a good idea. Let him know that you are in this for life, you are happy to give him his space to contemplate, *and you aren't going anywhere in the meantime.* You have plenty of time to leave if I am wrong."

When I feel myself trying to control a situation, I ask myself what I call the Five Fs of Powering Up—five questions that help me clarify my thinking. So I tried out the questions on Jane:

The first F stands for *factors.*

"What *factors* are you trying to control?" I asked.

Jane replied, "His decision about whether we get married."

"Can you control these factors?"

"I wish . . . but, of course not."

"Okay. So control is not an option."

The second F is *fear.* "What do you *fear?*"

"That's easy. I fear getting rejected. Again. He's not the only one who has had a failed relationship."

The third F is *focus.* "What's your *focus?*" (or, as our British friends would say, "What do you fancy?") In other words, what do you really want?

"I want to marry a wonderful man, have a family, and live happily ever after."

That leads us to the fourth F, *faith.* "What or whom do you have *faith* in?"

She said, "I believe things happen for a reason and that God has a plan for me."

"Okay, good. Now you have crystallized for yourself what's beyond your control, what you're afraid of, what you really want, and what you have faith in."

Now let's explore the fifth F, *facilitate.*

"How can you facilitate getting what you want? Will leaving him now help or hurt your chances? Think of your decision using the ABCs of power. How could you use your powers to *act, believe,* and *choose* to get what you want? Could you *act* so he knows you respect his emotional needs and appreciate his honesty, modeling for him how it will be when you get married? Can you *believe* that if he really does have doubts, getting married would not be a good idea anyway? Could you *choose* to support him by not filling in the blanks, give him the reasonable amount of time he has asked for, and then simply wait for him to make a decision?"

The long story made short is that she let go of her need to control the outcome, stopped filling in the blanks, and practiced patience. It took just a few days for her boyfriend to realize the only mistake he could make was not spending the rest of his life with this wonderful woman. The happily married couple just celebrated their fourth anniversary and their son's second birthday.

In the phrase "pause before judging," *pause* is the operative word. Many times things work out in our favor if we don't ruin them by overreacting to "facts" we have fabricated or going off on tangents that waste time and energy.

Try the Five Fs of Powering Up—factors, fear, focus, faith, and facilitate—the next time you feel yourself filling in the blanks. You may find that your decisions become easier and you move in a quicker, more direct path to reach your dreams.

Speed Minus Accuracy: A Business Formula for Disaster

Some might argue that because of the speed at which our business decisions need to be made, we have to fill in the blanks and just move forward. There's not always time to gather and recheck all the facts. But much of our business success depends on doing our job right the first time. Imagine if Domino's Pizza, which promised "30 minutes or it's on us," consistently brought you anchovy pizza when you ordered pepperoni. What if the pharmacist just assumed the prescription read *insulin* (a drug for diabetes) when the scrawled writing really said *Inderal* (a heart medicine)? What if she didn't want to take the time to call the physician for clarification? Everyone wants fast service, but no one wants *inaccurate* fast service.

Businesses can also suffer when we make assumptions about our coworkers. Filling in the blanks is so common at work that we hardly see it as such. We scarcely notice comments like, "I saw Roberta's husband lunching with his secretary three times this week. We all know what *that* means." "We're missing some petty cash again; both times were on Susan's shift. I guess she has some explaining to do." Even the most respected journalists in this country sometimes fall into this trap. Some of you may remember how quickly Richard Jewell, the security guard who found the bomb during the 1996 Olympics in Atlanta, went from hero to suspect. His life turned nightmarish as the whole world responded to the "news" of his guilt. Journalists jumped to conclusions, and we bought in because we wanted the crime solved. We gathered just enough evidence to make his guilt a certainty. "Knowing" who committed the crime made us all feel safe and in control again. The only problem was, *he didn't do it.*

Add to our need for speed the peer pressure of a mob mentality, and trouble builds. When the whole team starts to gather evidence to make a case against someone, we can find ourselves swept up and way down the wrong road without even realizing it. It's important for us to understand in those circumstances that ultimately the best power move may be to pause, back up, and change our course. I received a letter from Anne, who helped one company do just that, to everyone's benefit:

Dear Mary,

I was working with a bank in New York, doing regular team-building sessions with the regional directors. There was one guy whom no one really admired. He was overweight, always a little disheveled, and didn't seem to take his job quite as seriously as everyone else. The other regional managers began to resent his frequent sick days, and when he skipped the company picnic, they considered it evidence that he just didn't want to be a team player. To top it off, he went on vacation to Disney World during their busiest time. Resentments increased, and conversations behind his back centered on whether he ought to be on the team at all.

One day during our sessions, he asked if we could have lunch together. I wondered why but agreed. At lunch, he first asked that I agree not tell anyone what he was about to tell me, and then he told me his wife had AIDS and was dying. She had had it for several years from a blood transfusion given in an operation. The hospital had enrolled her in a program that cared for her up until the day after the statute of limitations for them to sue had expired. They were then left to finance treatment on their own. After a second mortgage on their home, they were in danger of losing it. They had tried to keep the AIDS diagnosis a secret, fearing the prejudice that they had already seen toward their children and from the people they thought were their friends. The trip to Disney World was expected to be the last vacation they took as a family.

My heart hurt for this strong, committed man who bore his burden in silence. I was able to convince him to give his team members a chance to rise to the occasion. After the way they had treated him lately, it wasn't easy, but he decided to try. After lunch, he told his story to the group. There were even a few tears. The group rallied around him and made sure people were available to help out when he needed to stay home. As a result, the entire group became closer and did more team building than any formal group process could have achieved. Both he and the group had jumped to conclusions that were very, very wrong. Once they gave each other a chance, they found a deeper connection that benefited all.

Sincerely,

Anne

Carelessly filling in the blanks can damage reputations, ruin marriages, and destroy careers. It might break a heart. As humans, we have the power to act in other ways—to understand the harm we can cause and guard against the nearly irresistible urge to make sense of senseless events by jumping to erroneous conclusions. We can choose to take our responsibility to pause before judging seriously.

> I love to quote Michael Annison, author of *Managing the Whirlwind,* who wrote, "If you are going in the wrong direction, speeding up doesn't help." He's right. Speed minus accuracy is rarely a formula for business success. Make sure pausing is part of your business formula. With that, you wield great power.

The 36-24-36 Rule

One day I received this e-mail from a friend:

> *I believe we should reinterpret silence in our society. You know how if we call someone and they don't call us back, we think they don't like us, or if we send someone a gift and they don't respond, we conclude that they didn't care for it? I think we should have the opposite response, like, "They are so thrilled and enchanted because I called that they can hardly believe it's true and will call when they come down from the state of euphoria that my call induced!" or "They are having such a good time with my gift that they cannot find significant enough words to express their gratitude." I mean, even if it's not true, it is just a nicer way to walk around thinking. This is my very roundabout way of saying I hope that you were engaging in*

such an interpretation and knew that I utterly loved my gift
from you before I found the words to describe it.

I laughed at her clever honesty but also found myself pondering her words of wisdom. Another woman confided, "My friend's sister is not a very attractive person, but she is convinced that she's strikingly gorgeous and that whenever someone is staring at her, they are just in awe of her good looks!" Why can't we all err on that side? If we're so naturally good at filling in the blanks, why do we so rarely fill them in with good stuff?

I catch myself filling in the blanks with an unnecessary negative tone too. I was commissioned to write an article for a national publication, and when I didn't hear from the editor two weeks after submitting my work, I was sure that he found my writing so appalling he didn't quite know how to break the bad news. This interpretation went against what I knew: it was a well-written, content-rich article. So why couldn't I conclude that the manuscript was just fine? I was afraid. I needed to prepare for rejection, lest I lose control. I finally got up the nerve to call and learned the article was accepted without revision and had already gone to press.

The next time you feel the urge to fill in the blanks to stem your craving for control, fill it in with good hunches. Here's a microaction to start with: Tell everyone that though you

and I have never met, you're pretty sure that I measure 36-24-36, have won a Pulitzer Prize for literature (or peace—you can decide), and I'm filthy rich. In fact, you read it somewhere.

Spread the word.

SHORTENING OUR LISTS ONCE AND FOR ALL

Filling in the blanks is an ineffective control technique; it overloads our schedules with "problems" that may never happen. We waste time when we have to redo our actions that were initially based on half-truths. We miss out on opportunities that could bring us joy. We risk hurting others deeply. As the old line reminds us, "Two wrongs are only the beginning." Pausing before judging is one of the most practical yet least practiced of all our powers. If we stop filling in the blanks, we'll clear our to-do list faster than any other strategy I can imagine, since much of its length comes from our unrealistic notion that being in the know means being in control.

TOOLS FOR YOUR REPAIR KIT
Slow Up!

1. Pause to ask, "Do I have all the facts, or have I presupposed some of the details?"

2. Get out of the lonely World According to Me.

3. Use the Five Fs of Powering Up:
   - What *factors* are you trying to control?

   - What do you *fear?*

   - What's your *focus?*

   - What or whom do you have *faith* in?

   - How could you *facilitate* reaching your goal using your powers to act, believe and choose?

4. Make accuracy part of your business formula for success.

5. Wield your power responsibly, because carelessly filling in the blanks can cause others irreversible damage.

6. Invoke the 36-24-36 rule. When you must fill in
    the blanks, fill them in positively.

POWER UP!
In Real Life

I know the person who wrote this letter. She is one of the
kindest, most generous and loving women I have ever met,
which serves to underscore how susceptible we all are.

Dear Mary,

*You need to know that you are onto something major with
this power of pausing before you judge. Here is what happened
to me today.*

*As soon as I walked into my yoga class, I noticed a beauti-
ful woman (about thirty years old) in the back of the class. She
had her hair in an updo ("A bit dressy for yoga," I thought) and
was dressed like a ballet dancer. She had a perfect body. I
glanced at her and thought, "That outfit tells me everything I
need to know about that woman." Throughout class, the
woman seemed to be able to do some quite difficult yoga moves
but needed the help of the bar or wall for some rather simple
ones. "She probably wrecked her body in ballet," I concluded to
myself. The teacher helped and corrected the woman several*

times (I figured she was sucking up). As the class ended, the instructor did not leave the room as is customary, but instead went over to help the woman again. It was at that moment I realized that the young woman was blind.

BLIND!

I had been silently, shallowly judging a woman for her physical beauty when she cannot even see how physically beautiful she is. I had been judging her physical limitations when she was doing a ninety-minute very challenging yoga class without the benefit of sight! As the instructor helped her into her taxicab, I could do nothing but sob. I was overcome by guilt and the knowledge that when I fill in the blanks, I am always, always wrong. Today marks the last day that I fill in the blanks. I realize that I cannot stop my mind from having the thoughts, but I can stop the thoughts midstream. Eventually, they will stop coming altogether, and I can dedicate that mindfulness to something useful and helpful.

A HOT FLASH OF POWER

Pause before you judge. You'll save yourself and others *untold*—in every sense—misery.

5

LOOK UP
Pay Attention

Picture this: I am in my kitchen simultaneously talking on the cordless phone to my mother, checking my business e-mail, watching TV to find out who wants to be a millionaire, doing my leg lifts, helping my son with his spelling words, microwaving pasta for dinner, unloading the dishwasher, pinching dead leaves off the geranium while making a mental note to water it more frequently, giving my teenaged daughter a big thumbs down to her request for a later curfew tonight and . . . on the fifty-sixth leg lift I remember I had to go to the bathroom four hours ago and still haven't taken a break.

We try very hard to handle our many demands by multitasking. Originally *multitasking* was the computer term for describing operating systems capable of running several applications at once. Now we use it to describe one of the most frequently used strategies for gaining control. Research by Yankelovich, Inc., bears this out. They found that 92 percent of women agreed with the statement, "I'm grateful to any product or brand that makes it easier for me to get several things done at the same time." Roseanne thinks Sears should invent a riding vacuum. I'm hoping someone will come out with an oven that can make toast, dry a load of towels, and heat my hair curlers on those mornings I am running late.

Eighty-seven percent of women agreed with the statement, "It seems I'm always doing more than one thing at a time." Think about our collective lifestyles. Nearly nine of every ten women in America are almost always doing two or more things simultaneously. Lest you think I exaggerate, tell me you don't know a woman who has applied makeup while driving. We are over the line.

Our feverish desire to multitask may be fueled in part by fear. Eighty-one percent of us said, "There seem to be more things to worry about than there were just a few years ago." As the world gets scarier, it makes sense to double our efforts to control.

It's That Corpus Callosum Again

We like to accomplish, and our brains are well equipped to do so. The Pulitzer Prize–winner Natalie Angier wrote in *Woman: An Intimate Geography,* that a "woman's mosaic brain" makes us consummate jugglers. In the book *EVEolu-tion,* the futurist Faith Popcorn explains that evolution may have selected our brains for this function. She wrote, "Certainly since pre–Stone Age, a millennium of conditioning has placed women in multiple positions. With their original responsibility being caretaker for the offspring, every other responsibility became an add-on, a simultaneous set of 'to-do's.' After all, if you put the baby down so that you can turn your attention to rubbing sticks together for a fire, a hungry mountain lion just might make the most of the opportunity. Can't do one thing; must do both. As if a life depended on it . . . multitasking has become a woman's survival response."

We *can* do fifty things at once and "save time," but is multitasking mania really an effective long-term survival response? As I stand in my kitchen in the midst of chaos, can I hear the fear in my mother's voice when she expresses concerns about paying for her heating bill? Can I read my client's e-mail well enough to recognize the faulty logic he's applied to the new project? Can I sense my teenager's anxiety about going to a late-night party where peer pressure is dangerously intense? I can see what I've accomplished on my to-do list, but can I see what I'm missing in my overstimulated state?

How can we drive attentively (efficiently grocery shop, enjoy the movie, or savor our meal while dining out) *and*

talk on a cell phone? The CEO of a large furniture manufac-
turer described his company's new chair that boasts a built-
in phone jack, an electrical outlet to plug in a laptop and
modem, and a swivel work tray to hold the computer. He
said, "We wanted to create something that could be used in
the living room, where people could spend time with their
families while working."

Huh? It's the *living* room, not the *working* room. Exactly
how do you spend time *with* your family when you are
wired to the rest of the world? Women will always multitask,
but if we continue to take our craving for control to such an
extreme, we will lose more than we gain.

We have to understand that when we let go of some
things, others automatically come into clearer focus. We
have to believe that Chicken Little's sky will not fall if we put
something down for a minute.

Our ability to pay attention is a power that draws others
to us. I chatted with Francis Weaver, author of *The Girls with
the Grandmother Faces,* who makes regular appearances on
NBC's *Today* show. I'm a secret Matt Lauer groupie, so I had
to know: "Tell me. What's he really like? I mean, is it just me,
or does every woman unconsciously start humming, 'You
can eat crackers in my bed any old time' whenever he comes
on the air?"

I will never forget her answer. Her seventy-plus-year-old eyes turned serious as she said, "He really pays attention to you." She didn't mention he is a top-rated TV personality, talented interviewer, and respected journalist. She seemed oblivious to my joking remarks about his drop-dead gorgeous appearance. His most impressive characteristic was that he *paid attention* to her. All I could think of was, "How do I get on his show?"

People love attention. In a way, it's all we really have to offer one another. How else do we let them know they are interesting, cared for, funny, and desired?

The poet William Meredith said that the worst that can be said of a person is that they "did not pay attention." So maybe the converse holds true as well: The *best* that can be said of a woman is that she did pay attention. Here are some things to think about to help you focus on what is really important.

The Eyes Have It

"There is no one way to raise a child," according to the National Longitudinal Study on Adolescent Health. This landmark $25 million two-year study concluded that all you have to do is "love, understand and pay attention" to your child. I think the women in my old bowling league concluded that one day. If they'd asked, we would have told them that for half the money and in a lot less time. But although we intuitively know that paying attention is the ultimate parenting tool, we underutilize it. One mother confessed to me, "I was in the kitchen after work, racing around doing five hundred things at once just like you're describing, and after several attempts to tell me about her school day, my five-year-old daughter put her little hands on both of my cheeks, turned my face to hers, and sputtered, 'Mommy! Listen to me with your eyes.' "

Georgia O'Keeffe said, "Seeing takes time." You might be thinking, "But I don't have time right now." I know. But when will we? Are we really willing to accept a life that has no time to see? Everyone benefits if we occasionally let go of our super-efficacy and take the time to look.

I learned a simple lesson on a freezing cold Saturday morning in February about how much our kids want our undivided attention.

It's 8:00 A.M. and so cold in Colorado I can see my breath. I can't feel my toes. I am standing on the sidelines of the snow-covered soccer field watching my son, Nicholas, and his teammates kick a rock-hard ball over the frozen ground. The other team, believe it or not, is wearing shorts. It makes me question whether I have suddenly lost ten IQ points and am no longer smart enough, as we used to say in Iowa, to come in out of the rain. The boys look over at the sidelines, certain some parent will step forward and order us all back to our warm beds.

As the team advances toward the goal, the parents shout encouragement: *Let's go, Justin! Let's go, Jeremy! Let's go, Michael!* I'm standing there mummy-wrapped in a blanket thinking, "Let's go . . . home!"

At half-time, I bolt for the car, turn on the heater full blast, and try to retain enough heat to tide me over for thirty more minutes.

I see the game begin again and trudge down the hill to the field. Nick approaches me on the sidelines as I come walking back.

"Did you leave?" he asks.

"No, of course not. I just warmed up in the car."

"Did you watch the first half?"

"Yes."

"Are you going to stay on the field for the second half?"

I tried to figure out what he was really asking. It finally dawned on me: he just wanted me to *pay attention.* Forget about being cold. Forget that I know only one rule about soccer (the ball in their goal is good and in our goal is bad). He wanted me to *watch* him. Kids know we're imperfect; they simply want us fully present. They need us to spend time looking at them, just unifocused, uninterrupted looking . . . without a cell phone.

It's not just kids who want to be "eyed." I asked an audience to relate their most romantic experience. One woman described the day her sister got married: "I was the maid of honor, and as I walked down the aisle, my boyfriend just lit up when he saw me. As my sister entered the church in her beautiful white gown on my father's arm, the entire congregation stood and turned to her—all of them except my boyfriend. He could not take his eyes off me. He stood there watching me the entire time. I have never felt so loved in all my life."

> Marcel Proust said, "The real voyage of discovery consists not in seeking new landscapes, but in having new eyes." Those peepers create enormous power. Look up and listen with your eyes.

Only Your Hairdresser Knows for Sure

Do you ever find yourself confiding in a stranger (maybe a taxicab driver) or your hairdresser, sharing details you might not tell others? One ingenious mother capitalized on this common phenomenon. The mother of twin girls, Linda Steinbach wanted an easy way to reopen the lines of communication with her girls at the end of the day. The standard question, "How was school today?" was met with the standard response, "Fine." So she invented a character they could talk to. When she wants to pay attention to her daughters, she becomes Josephine the manicurist. One on one, she sits down and soaks, files, buffs, and paints each girl's nails. The two converse as if they are in a salon. "Hi, I'm Josephine, and I will be your manicurist. What's your name?" Josephine peppers the conversation with questions: "What is the worst thing about second grade?" "Tell me about your best friend." "What is your favorite subject?" "What worries you about growing up?" This clever mother beamed when she told me, "My girls sing like canaries! I learn so much by listening and just paying attention to them that they don't seem to mind the occasional bits of wisdom from their manicurist. Whenever I feel the urge to connect with them, I let Josephine open the doors."

Linda has created more than just a way to find out about her children's lives without grilling them: She has established a lifelong communication pathway. My guess is that when her grown daughters face a challenge—a failed love relationship, a family conflict, a major disappointment at work—they will call their mom and say, "Does Josephine have any openings today?"

SITTING DOWN FOR A CURE

I love the Josephine approach, and the scientist in me always wonders why such behaviors work so well. Dr. David

Lickerman, associate director of emergency medicine at Christian Hospitals in St. Louis, writes courses for doctors. His findings may explain Josephine's effectiveness. He discovered, for example, that a doctor who sits down with a patient doubles the time the patient perceives the doctor has spent with him. I had to sit down when I read that. So for all the effort I put into making my relationships good ones, I could just sit down, and my family would perceive that I have spent twice as long with them? This was important news I could use. Another survey by health care researchers showed that when a doctor asks a patient what is wrong, the average time that patient has to respond before the doctor interrupts is eighteen seconds. "Doctors want to seize control of the conversation and lead the patient down the path of medical inquiry," Lickerman told a *St. Louis Dispatch* reporter. "Giving up control, even for little while, needs to be taught to physicians."

Might this advice also apply to us? When we ask our child or partner a question, do we give that person more than eighteen seconds before we jump in to offer advice, reprimand, or solve the problem? Maybe we don't interrupt to control, but just like the physicians, we receive only part of the story and send the message that we're in charge.

SMALL TALK WITH BIG RESULTS

Sitting down for a chat can have a deep impact. A study in the December 2000 issue of *Psychology of Addictive Behavior* found that a talk between mother and teenager can help prevent binge drinking by college freshmen. Students who said they had a conversation with their mothers "about how drinking can get me into trouble and is bad for my health" were less likely to drink excessively than students who said they consumed alcohol because "it was a nice way to celebrate special occasions" or "it made it easier to talk to people." As parents, we may think that our children already know the vices to avoid, so why lecture? We don't need to harp, but paying just a little attention to the topics goes a long way in helping our children resist temptation.

The columnist Ellen Goodman wrote, "Ultimately there is no way to do one minute mothering. There is no way to pay attention in a hurry." So take the time to sit down. It's a simple microaction, and the rewards could be huge. It might cure what's wrong while it doubles the time you spend on what's really important in life.

Leaping Cowboys

I had the honor of speaking at the National Country Music Radio convention in Nashville, where Garth Brooks, country music's megastar, delivered the keynote address. Garth spoke to the audience sitting on a stool at center stage and answering questions. The emcee's first question was, "Garth, you will host the *Saturday Night Live* TV show in a few days, and your contract requires you to stay in New York City and rehearse all week. In addition, last night you performed, presented, and received an award at the Grammys. Neither SNL nor your recording company wanted you to leave town. So why are you here?"

He smiled. "First of all, I said I would come, and I keep my word. Secondly, I have not forgotten that country music radio *made* Garth Brooks. I wanted to be here with you."

After his address, the emcee offered the 3,100 attending disc jockeys, program directors, and station owners an opportunity to ask Garth a question. Several raced to the center microphone. After a few minutes, the emcee thanked Garth for coming and said to him, "It is time for you to go back for rehearsals."

Garth pointed to the center microphone and replied, "I'm going to fly back to New York, but *first,* I'm going to answer the questions of these seven people still in line."

After he addressed four more attendees the emcee again urged, "Garth, I am getting the word that jet fuel is very expensive and the plane is revved up and ready to take you back to. . . ."

Garth politely broke in and said, "I'm going to leave. But *first* I want to answer the last three people still in line."

The first man had "a two-part question." I cringed at his insensitivity, but Garth did not seem a bit concerned, answering both inquiries. The next man made an equally complicated request, and unfazed, Garth granted his wish too.

The last person in line was one of the few women in the audience. She shyly said, "Garth, I don't have a question, but I came all the way from Alaska. Our station has sponsored several of your concerts, and even though I've been backstage with you, I have never had the opportunity to shake your hand. I don't want to get this close and miss out again. All I want is a handshake."

Garth grinned, slowly took off his big black cowboy hat, leaped off the stage, and ran full speed down the center aisle. He swept the woman off her feet and gave her a huge bear hug.

You could have heard a pin drop. I looked around the room and saw 3,100 men clearly touched, many wiping away tears. When we poured out of the ballroom, I heard them murmur, "Genuine, real, down-to-earth, authentic."

Why was this such a magical moment? Why were these men as impressed with Garth's display of affection as they were with his phenomenal recording success? Garth wowed them by giving his audience a few extra minutes of his time, showing them respect, and expressing interest in meeting their needs. He simply paid attention to them.

Some may wonder if his behavior was merely a marketing strategy. I don't think it was, and the people I talked to certainly didn't see it that way. In addition, Garth Brooks's CD sales that year accounted for nearly 20 percent of all country music CDs sold. A megastar of his caliber could have gone back to New York early and still had record sales. But even if it was somehow a strategic move, it simply underscores the power of paying attention in business. Do you think I am the only one telling this story? Would you be surprised if thousands of deejays recounted the tale of Garth's kindness and then played his CD as a follow-up? Garth Brooks illustrates the energy we create in both business and personal lives when we give someone our undivided attention.

What about your "audience"? Often the greater the distance in the hierarchy—celebrity to fan, parent to child, fortunate to less fortunate—the greater the impact we have. Do not underestimate your ability to affect others positively simply

by paying attention. To whom do you need to pay attention? Make a list and jot the names in your datebook or some other easy-to-reach place. Try the microaction of just reading those names several times a day.

A Midlife Treasure Hunt

When I was thirty-six years old, I had a midlife crisis. (Some of you may be thinking, "But thirty-six is not really midlife." Well, I have always been an overachiever, so I had it early. In fact, I liked it so much I've had a few more since.) It was one of those "I need to find myself" crises that drives even the sanest crazy for a while. After finishing a graduate degree, establishing a career, giving birth to three children, and devoting my life to babies and then preschoolers, my husband, and his elderly parents, I wondered, "What about Mary?" I became quite narcissistic, the hallmark of a really good midlife crisis. My new independent behavior was especially worrisome to my husband, because many of our friends were going through similar experiences and were getting divorced faster than you can say, "I do—not." I tried to reassure him that my insanity was undoubtedly benign and temporary, but try as he might, he could not understand my unrest. Our close relationship started to unravel.

He remained worried until the night I sent our three children to a friend's house for the evening. I left Joe a note asking him to prepare for a very special night and then to drive to his health club. As he checked in, the receptionist handed him an envelope with a note that read,

> *Dear Joe,*
>
> *I appreciate how hard you work to stay healthy and fit. I'm grateful that you get up at 5:30 in the morning to work out so you can spend evenings with us. I love your body . . . [imagine a bunch of really juicy stuff here]. Now go to Joyce's house.*
>
> *Love,*
>
> *Mary*

Joyce waited patiently with the envelope I had dropped off. It said,

> *Joyce came to our wedding over thirteen years ago. There was never a bride more sure of what she was doing when she walked down that aisle, and that bride has not changed her mind. Now go to the gazebo in Washington Park.*

In the park, I had found a young security guard in dress blues who was watching over a wedding reception. I explained my mission to him, and he assured me he would stay no matter what time my husband arrived. He proudly handed the note to Joe a few hours later:

Dear Honey,

> *This is the park where we walked as young lovers, planned our life together, and strolled our babies. We solved a lot of problems here. Now go to 837 South Williams and look under the planter.*

This was the address of our first house. Joe had built a planter that still stood on the front porch. Under it I nestled the next note:

Dear Joe,

> *We began our married life here. On the day we brought our first child home, you insisted on carrying her "over the threshold." But when I went into the house and looked back, the two of you had vanished. I finally spied you in the garage, showing a two-day-old baby your boat and explaining how you would someday teach her to water ski! You have been a wonderful father ever since and—she water-skis beautifully. Now go to the site of our first date fifteen years ago.*

He arrived at the Riviera restaurant, a Mexican diner, and there I sat. Although he's not one to cry, he smiled at me with tears in his eyes and said, "I guess our roots go pretty deep. I can see we have solved a lot of problems in the past. I think you've showed me what you've been trying to tell me. Maybe we should sit down and talk about our concerns."

My little treasure hunt, as he calls it, did not solve our problems. We still had issues to resolve. But instead of trying to control each other in a debate of who was right or wrong, we paid attention to what we really had and it put us in the right frame of mind to work on our marriage.

You too might one day find yourself in the throes of a midlife crisis or a major career move. Perhaps you're struggling with a house full of toddlers or teenagers or, God forbid, both. As a result, your other relationships could be in need of repair. Remember: You won't get all the work done anyway, so pay attention to the people you love. Let go of the to-do list from time to time. Focus on the power of what you already have. You won't regret it.

Paying "Intention"

As I travel the world, I meet people who constantly amaze me with their resourcefulness. Doug Parks at the Mayo Clinic wrote to me:

Dear Mary,

I have found that paying attention can be taken to the next level by something I call "paying intention." It's more proactive than attention, which can be a reaction or a response to someone else. You actually seek someone out with the idea of giving them undivided presence and love.

Today's families are especially creative when it comes to paying intention. Here are five of my favorite examples:

Julie and Brad Mitchell of Virginia are like many other families, apart more than they'd like because of long work hours and travel demands. They wanted to let their children know that their family was first in their hearts, so they established a national holiday for their family. March 1 is officially Mitchell Day. They spend the entire day enjoying activities that celebrate the fact that they belong to each other.

Carrianne, from Hawaii, pays intention with a unique photo swap. She said, "My best friend and I graduated from college in 1986. I had a favorite picture of the two of us that I put in a card to her about ten years ago with a note that read: 'Every time I see this picture of the two of us, it reminds me of all the wonderful fun we have shared and how much you mean to me. Let's pass this picture between the two of us for the rest of our lives.' Now, when either of us least expects it, the photo will 'come back.' Sometimes a few years go by, but it will always come back."

Gwyneth Jones of Missouri told me how unsatisfying it is for a single woman to eat alone each night. She said her motivation to set the table and prepare a nice meal deteriorated into eating off a paper plate standing at the counter. So she pays a little intention. Once a month, she and her friend in another state set a "date" for dinner. Out come the china, fine linens, favorite recipes, soft music, and candlelight. Then they both get on speaker phone and dine "together," describing all the loveliness around them.

Instead of being overwhelmed with the demands of a child with special needs and an aging parent, Jeanette Whiteman of New Jersey used her power of paying intention. She wrote:

My six year old takes therapeutic horseback riding lessons on Saturday mornings as a treatment modality for cerebral palsy. My seventy-four-year-old father also has grown to expect my time on Saturday mornings. So to combat this dilemma, I asked him to go to Nicole's horseback lesson with us. He absolutely loved it and was so proud and astonished that Nicole could sit up so well on a horse when she can't sit very well in a chair. She is so excited when Grandpop comes to watch her that she tries even harder to do well. He has grown to expect this time with the two of us, as have we. In fact, last week, he said he couldn't go, so off we went by ourselves. (Of course, when we got home, we found out that he had arrived at our house only minutes after we had left and stayed there, waiting for us, disappointed we didn't foresee his change of mind!) Now we have it understood: that we will go to class weekly as three generations.

Adolescents often struggle with their rapidly changing body image. Cathy Parsell addressed this common problem by letting go and refocusing the intention. She wrote,

> *Dear Mary,*
>
> *My eighth-grade daughter was constantly complaining about the way she looked. Her hair was too dull, her ears too big, her second toe too long. I was tired of it. I said, "No more!" I asked her to write down her complaints whenever she thought of them, and I would listen to them on the tenth of every month.*
>
> *The tenth of the month came, and sure enough, she had a lengthy list. When she was finished reading it, I went to the drawer and pulled out the list I had been working on. Mine was a list of all the things I liked about her.*

Julie, Carrianne, Gwyneth, Jeanette, and Cathy did not try to control long working hours, distance, marital status, family demands, or insecure teenagers. They all very cleverly found a way to let go and then do everything in their power by paying intention.

Paying intention, a creatively proactive approach to giving someone your undivided presence and love, multiplies your power again and again. What one microaction could you take to be more intentional?

Give Yourself Credit

It's easier to power up if we acknowledge our efforts and give ourselves credit for a job well done. One woman told me about the guilt she felt as a young, single mom of three little ones. Despite working long and hard, her budget rarely stretched far enough to meet even the most basic needs like breakfast cereal or birthday presents. To compensate, she gave her children a box of cereal wrapped in old newspapers each year for their birthday. She said her heart sank at the thought of this crude annual gift. But surprisingly, even as her financial picture improved, her kids reminded her as their birthdays grew near: "Don't forget to wrap up my box of cereal." She had no idea of its significance until she attended her three-year-old granddaughter's birthday party. Among the gifts was a box of cereal wrapped in old newspapers. Her daughter beamed, "It always meant love to us, Mom. I want to pass it on."

The best attention is not necessarily expensive or elaborate. Let it simply pour from your heart, and then give yourself credit for all the little things that say, "I noticed you."

There Really Is Too Much to Do

Even if we could do one hundred things at the same time, we still wouldn't get everything done in our lifetime. There will always be more paperwork than we can efficiently shuffle, more housework than we can accomplish, and more needs than any woman could humanly meet. We won't stop feeling overwhelmed until we allow ourselves to feel underwhelmed: Stop. Look. Listen. Paying attention is a power that can make us miracle workers. Tap into it.

TOOLS FOR YOUR REPAIR KIT
Look Up!

1. Listen with your eyes.

2. Double your time by sitting down.

3. Identify who needs your attention and be aware of the distance of that person from you in the hierarchy.

4. In difficult times, pay attention to the people you love and the power of what you have together.

5. Invent creative ways to pay intention.

6. Give from the heart, and then give yourself credit for all the good you do.

POWER UP!
In Real Life

Dear Mary,

One day in November, my life changed. I ran to my car after work because I was late, and my day care provider prefers the kids to be picked up by 6:00 P.M. This was not unusual for me to be racing to her house. It was a bit icy, which threw my schedule off as I had to slow down. I got there at 6:10 P.M., ran into the house, quickly got the kids' shoes and coats on, and said, "Come on, boys, we have to hurry because Mom has a meeting at 6:30." Benjamin is three, and Nicholaus is six. We ran to the car, and both boys, who are quite independent, got in by themselves and as usual buckled up on their own. The doors shut, and I put the car in reverse. At that exact second, Nicholaus screamed from the back seat, "Mom! Benjamin!" I put on the brakes and looked back. Benjamin's door was open! He had slipped and fallen under the car. He was lying right next to the front tire of the driver's side—so close that his coat was caught under the tire. I almost ran over my own son!

I lost it like never before. I realized at that moment that my life had to change.

Sincerely,

Rhonda Jolliffe

A HOT FLASH OF POWER

Pay attention. Listen with your eyes, give from your heart, and stage a sit-in.

6

LISTEN UP
Pose Good Questions

Real life is not neat; it's full of ironies, inconsistencies, injustices, and pain. Our tendency in those situations is to squeeze even tighter in an attempt to get a grip on our problems. When we're stressed, we sometimes ask the wrong questions (e.g., "Why don't *they* do something?"), or we stop making inquiries altogether. One of the most important tools we have in our repair kit is our ability to ask good questions.

I sent surveys to my readers and inquired, "What good questions do you ask yourself when you're stressed out or feeling a great loss?" As always, my readers were ingenious. I selected six questions that I believe are incredibly useful in helping us power up.

Here are six Things to Think About.

Question 1: Is This Really a Crisis?

Our control radar screen goes crazy the instant we think we have a crisis to prevent or solve. But is it really a crisis we're dealing with? How do we define *crisis?*

DOES IT AFFECT YOUR BREATHING?

I was helping a manager of a large restaurant chain with her own life balance issues. She said, "I can't ever have a moment to myself because even when I take time off, my employees call me at home. To them, everything is an emergency. I have to drive back to the restaurant and solve the problem. I don't want to be in charge of everything. How do I get them to let go so I can too?"

I told her about the time my husband went into a windshield replacement store. Now imagine the receptionist, a thin, wiry-looking woman in her thirties, sitting behind her desk. A customer is chewing her out royally, raising his voice, and threatening to sue, and eventually he stomps out and slams the door behind him. The woman, completely unruffled, smiles at my husband and says sweetly, "May I help you?"

Joe smiles back. "Gee, I want to compliment you on how you handled that little crisis."

She laughs. "In this business, I have learned that if it doesn't affect my breathing, I don't consider it a crisis."

I love that line and offered it to this manager. "Could you teach your employees to identify a crisis in this way? Tell them, 'If it does not affect your breathing, then it's not an emergency and you shouldn't call me. If the french-fry grease catches on fire, the kitchen will be smoky and it will affect your breathing. Call me. If we get robbed, you will be hyperventilating. Call me. If six tour buses stop and you are racing around to fill the orders, you will be panting. Call me. If you are breathing just fine, it is not a crisis, and I will expect you to deal with the problem until I return this afternoon.' "

CAN IT WAIT?

According to lore, Winston Churchill had a definition for crisis. The story goes that Churchill was a napper and hired a young aide to be his gatekeeper. He told the young man, "From time to time, I like to take a brief nap. It's never more than about fifteen or twenty minutes, but it really rejuvenates me. When I am napping I am not to be disturbed unless there is a crisis." The young man said, "Very good, sir." Churchill said, "No, not very good. Everyone who comes to you will tell you that what they have is a potential crisis, so I am going to tell you what a crisis is. It is armed invasion of the British Isles. Anything less than that can wait."

The management guru Peter Drucker put crisis in a similar perspective in his book *The Effective Executive*. He consulted once a month for two years with the president of a big bank. During the one-and-a-half-hour appointment, there was never a phone call or an interruption from the president's secretary. One day, Peter asked him about this. He answered, "My secretary has strict instructions not to put anyone through except the president of the United States and my wife. The president rarely calls. Everything else the secretary holds until I have finished. Then I have half an hour in which to return every call and make sure I get every message. I have yet to come across a crisis that could not wait ninety minutes." According to Drucker, this president got more accomplished in one session than many other equally capable executives do in a month of meetings, all because he understood the definition of a crisis.

The next time you are tempted to go into control mode over something fairly trivial, ask yourself, "Is this an armed invasion of the British Isles? Does it affect my breathing? Do I need to respond immediately?" Clarifying the definition will lower your stress, and with fewer events qualifying as crises, you'll have less to control.

Question 2: What Would My Role Model Do?

When I am at my wit's end, I ask myself, "What would Mary Benirschke do?" I met Mary more than ten years ago, but I remember it as if it was yesterday. I recall seeing her from afar, looking radiantly beautiful. Since then, in our time together, I know that beyond her beauty is an amazing reservoir of warmth, kindness, courage, and intelligence. I've watched how she lives her life with an enviable grace and style. She taught me about faith as she triumphed over tragedy and loss and about hope as she and her husband created a beautiful family with four children. I am not trying to *be* her; I'm trying to remind myself how I would like to behave. By asking this simple question, What would my role model do? I redirect my energy toward something positive.

The late Payne Stewart, a much beloved professional golfer, wore a bracelet that said, "What would Jesus do?" Other respondents told me they ask how their mother, grandmother, or other respected elder would have acted. Last summer, I met two role models for my business, Life Balance, Inc. In awe I watched Craig Fuller, president and CEO of the National Chain Drug Store Association, lead his organization with a compelling kindness that is difficult to describe—a sort of benevolent yet intensely powerful pied piper leadership style that empowers both optimist and cynic alike. I also observed John Young, the worldwide director of the Four Seasons Hotel, treat every guest like royalty. Julia Roberts was staying at the hotel at the time of my visit, and I can't imagine what he could have done to make her stay more comfortable than he made mine. (Well, okay, she probably had dinner with Brad Pitt and I didn't, but that was the only difference.) My business standards at Life Balance, Inc. are now gauged on asking, "What would Craig or John do?"

Who are your role models? What characteristics do you admire in them? How could you emulate their good qualities? How do they power up?

Question 3: What's So Funny?

One of the first things to go out the window when we're overwhelmed with a sense of responsibility is our sense of humor. Karyn Buxman, author of *"This Won't Hurt a Bit" and Other Fractured Truths in Healthcare,* is a master at finding humor amid chaos. An expert on the healing power of humor, her skills were put to good use one year when her ten-year-old son, Adam, went through months of tests at the best hospitals nationwide while doctors tried to find an effective treatment for his intractable headache disorder.

She asked her friends to send funny e-mails to keep her spirits up. Her replies were a hoot, and despite the seriousness of her child's illness, I looked forward to her updates on Adam's condition because they made me laugh. When I sent her an e-mail telling her I would throw up a prayer for Adam's recovery, she responded, "Please do not say, 'Throw up.' We have plenty of that already."

One day she described her son's visit to a highly specialized pediatric neurologist. He asked Adam, "Have you ever experienced déjà-vu?" Without missing a beat, her son volleyed back, "Haven't you asked me that question before?" Both Karyn and Adam dealt with uncertainty and suffering in a most impressive way.

I asked Karyn about the importance of using humor to help us let go of our need to control everything and enjoy life. She said, "When we're honest with ourselves, we realize that we have little or no control over much of what happens in our lives. But we do have a choice in how we respond to those events. We need a variety of tools to cope in a healthy manner, and one of the most powerful is humor. It's my personal bias that most humor comes from pain and discomfort—yours or someone else's. Sometimes it's from a big pain, sometimes it's from a minor discomfort—but face it—we're not laughing about a perfectly good hair day or sexy hips. Humor provides us with perspective. It gives us the ability to let go, detach ourselves from our pain, then twist it, turn it, and tweak it until we can eventually see it from a less painful and perhaps even funny point of view. I think humor and laughter are two of the greatest gifts God gave mankind. Never leave home without them!"

Some of you may be saying, "But what if I'm not all that funny?" (or as one woman put it, "Stop by *my* office. I dare you to find something funny!"). Dr. Michelle G. Newman, an assistant professor of psychology at Pennsylvania State University, studied the use of humor as a coping mechanism for stress. She found that humor can function as a positive coping strategy for everyone, even those who do not typically use it. Fortunately, other people don't necessarily need to think you are funny. She said, "From the standpoint of coping, it's less important whether you can amuse other people than whether you can amuse yourself."

Put those humor lenses on, and the next time you feel frustration building, ask yourself, "What's so funny?" Practice your skills when you're not going nuts so you'll be ready when the big test comes. One of the best microactions to use is to just watch people. We are the funniest species on earth. It won't be long before something strikes you as hilarious and you'll start to be more in tune with the humor in every day life.

Question 4: What Will This Decision Accomplish?

I like this question because although it will work in any area of your life, it especially helps parents move from "control over" to "power with" their kids. If you are having a hard time deciding how to discipline your child, consider each option and ask, "What will this accomplish?"

I was in my home office Saturday morning catching up on a few loose ends before I took the weekend off. Earlier that morning, I had noticed fourteen-year-old Emily and her older sister, Sarah, whispering. Emily came into my office and said, "I want to tell you something."

I looked up. "Sure. What is it?"

The tears flowed. I took her hand, and we snuggled on the sofa together. "I'm listening."

Her lip trembled. "Last night, Lisa and I were at Michelle's house. Lisa decided to bring a bottle of wine from her parents' wine cellar. We had planned to come over here while you were out for dinner and have our first taste of wine. Lisa's mom picked us up, and when we walked to the car, the bottle of wine must have dropped out of the sleeping bag where we'd hidden it, and it fell onto the front lawn. When we arrived at our house and found the bottle missing, my friends asked me if I could get some vodka from our liquor cabinet. Sarah overheard us talking and told us that we were out of our minds. She said we would get sick, you and Dad would find out, and we would get in big trouble. We got scared and decided it wouldn't be worth the risk. But someone found the wine on the lawn and told Lisa's mom. She figured it all out, and now I feel terrible."

I let her cry for a while. Then I asked, "So what are you feeling?"

"I feel guilty for going along with the plan to steal the wine. I was so stupid. I don't know how I will face Lisa's mom. I know you probably don't trust me now. I wasn't the one who took the wine, but I am in just as much trouble as my friends are. That's not fair."

"You have just learned one of the lessons of being a grown-up. You are responsible for who you hang out with because you're guilty by association. The guy who drives the getaway car gets charged with armed robbery just like the guy holding the gun and putting the money in the bag does. It may not seem fair, but it is how the grown-up world works. That's why it is important to choose your friends carefully and make good decisions."

She sobbed. "You know, Mom, the thrill of drinking is not worth the pain of getting caught. I feel so guilty."

We snuggled for a while longer, and then Emily called Lisa's mom to apologize.

So here is the sixty-four-dollar question: Do I punish her? I recognize that most children are curious about and experiment with alcohol. On the other hand, stealing is a crime, underage drinking is dangerous, not to mention illegal, and violating someone's trust has consequences. But if I ground her, fine her, or give her more chores to do, what will it accomplish? I decided not to punish her because when I asked the question, I could not find a satisfactory answer. I felt she had learned a valuable lesson, her conscience was punishing her already, and I wanted to reward her courage for telling me the truth on her own. She learned to accept responsibility, deal with shame, and apologize. What was she going to gain by sitting in her room for a week?

Two years later, Emily caused a fender bender a month after she got her license. She joined a big club—three out of five sixteen year olds have an accident the first year of driving. Fortunately, no one was injured, although our insurance premiums suffered extensive damage. There were consequences. Emily got a job to pay for the deductible, and she wrote a letter of apology to the other driver. What will *that* accomplish? Instead of being punished, she experienced what happens in the real world, a valuable bit of information I'm sure she has carefully filed away.

Perhaps you would have handled these situations differently. I don't think there is a right approach for all children.

I do believe, however, that asking the question "What will this decision *really* accomplish?" can help you hone in on your power and clarify the best course of action.

Look for opportunities to ask, "What will this decision accomplish?" What are you trying to achieve? Will your decision get you closer to or further away from the outcome you want? This process will give you insight into the best ways to act, believe, and choose.

Question 5: Why *Not* Me?

When we have a major loss in our lives, a natural response is to ask, "Why me?" Our lives have been turned upside down, and we want to make some sense of the upheaval and regain a sense of control. Unfortunately "Why me?" is an endless loop question that impedes our ability to power up and heal.

I received this unforgettable letter and later substantiated the remarkable story:

Dear Mary,

As someone who understands the importance of asking better questions, I'd like to share with you how changing what I said to myself saved my life. I had so many bad things happen to me, and with each loss I would ask, "Why me?" until that simple question turned into a tape that ran constantly over and over in my head. I'm not exaggerating when I say my life was full of negative events. My father died when I was eight years old. I was raped in high school by a popular athletic coach. I married at twenty-five and divorced soon after when I learned of my husband's extramarital affair. A car accident left me with a closed-head injury, and I spent over a year in occupational and speech therapy. I wondered if this black cloud would ever leave me.

My luck started to change when I received a decent settlement from the accident, and I moved to Nevada to be near my new fiancé. Because of my cash settlement, we were able to pay off all debt, buy new furniture, and purchase a new car for my husband-to-be. We even had money in the bank. Eight days before our wedding, I returned home from work to find an empty house. I would soon learn that my fiancé had run off to marry a coworker, taking everything, including all the money. How could so much happen to one person! What had I done to deserve this? Why me? This self-defeating question threw me into a huge black hole that I was sure would swallow me. When it didn't, I tried to take my own life.

Then one day, while talking with a close family friend, I asked my favorite question out loud. His answer infuriated me. "Why not you?"

Why not me! I stormed out, but it didn't take too long for his words to sink in and for me to realize that he couldn't be more right. Why not me? I didn't have to look far to see that everyone endures pain at some point in life. I have a stepsister who lost her vision at thirty. My grandmother buried both of her children at young ages. In fact, the man who shared his wisdom watched his wife suffer greatly after a brain aneurysm. No one has cornered the market on sorrow or loss.

"Why not me?" did not end my suffering, but it took the self-pity out of my pain—and it was the self-pity that was keeping me immobilized. But now with my new question, I have a better perspective. I finally understand that what I say to myself is powerful!

In closing, I've included a picture [see opposite] of my wonderful husband and me on our honeymoon, proving that there is a place for "Why not me?" in our pursuit of success and happiness!

Happily ever after,

Lacy Matthews

Gerald Sittser wrote the wonderful book *A Grace Disguised*. In his chapter entitled "Why *Not* Me? he wrote, "Most of us want to have control over our lives. . . . Loss deprives us of control. . . . Most of us want life not only to be under our control but also to be fair. So when we suffer loss we

claim our right to justice and resent circumstances that get in the way. We demand to live in a society in which virtue is rewarded and vice punished, hard work succeeds and laziness fails, decency wins and meanness loses." He concludes that since much of life seems just to happen beyond our control, "Why *not* me? seems as good a question to ask as any." He continues:

No one gets out of this world without experiencing loss. In our unpredictable, unjust, painful world, we find no reason that some people suffer and others don't. Loss has little to do with fairness. Asking "Why me?" implies that we should somehow be immune to the reality facing every other human on the planet. "Why *not* me?" is a question designed to allow you to power up when you need it most.

Question 6: Where Is God in All This?

Harold Kushner, author of the best-seller *When Bad Things Happen to Good People,* wrote the book to quell his "deep aching sense of unfairness" when his son died and to help others understand and overcome their anger at God for letting such tragic events occur. He encourages us to ask power questions. Instead of asking, "God, why are you doing this to me?" he suggests we ask, "God, see what is happening to me? Can you help?"

Death will always be one of the great human mysteries. Rabbi Kushner wrote, "We can't control it, or sometimes even postpone it." He concludes, "The God I believe in does not send us the problem. He gives us the strength to cope with the problem."

We can ask good questions, but often there's no good answer. The older we get, the more we come to terms with the simple fact that for some questions, there are never going to be answers. And perhaps, as Gertrude Stein wrote, "That's the answer."

Life is a mystery. Our ever-present challenge is to accept that. What questions do you ask your higher power?

How About You?

In response to my survey, I received dozens of other terrific ideas. One woman cleverly cautioned that if you seek outside advice to be sure to ask the right person. I know quite well what she is talking about. My husband often accuses me of misdirecting my queries by asking him things he could not possibly know. For example, I'll stand in the kitchen holding two pieces of burned toast, turn to him, and ask, "Why doesn't our toaster work?" He will look up from his bowl of cereal and grin, "Hon, I appreciate your confidence in me, but I have a master's degree in psychology. Do I look like a small-appliance repairman? I have no idea why the toaster won't toast." His point is well taken. Consider the source when you ask a question. Another woman wrote that she always asks, "Am I doing this solely to impress someone?" She explained, "This question usually comes up when I'm freaking out while scrubbing the toilet bowl five minutes before company is due or choking on carpet cleaner that I'm vacuuming out of the stained green shag carpeting."

You may have an entirely different set of questions that move you from striving for control to thriving with power. Write them down. Talk about them. Practice asking them aloud. In *Letters to a Young Poet,* Rainer Maria Rilke wrote, "I want to beg you as much as I can . . . to be patient toward all that is unsolved in your heart and to try to love the *questions themselves* like locked rooms and like books that are written in a very foreign tongue."

Love your questions, ask them often, and fill up with energy.

TOOLS FOR YOUR REPAIR KIT
Listen Up!

1. Understand your definition of a crisis.

2. Identify your role model and consider what he or she would do under similar circumstances.

3. Use humor to let go of your need to control.

4. Look for opportunities to ask, "What will this decision accomplish?"

5. Change your question from Why me? to Why *not* me? and power up when you need it most.

6. Ask God for strength to cope with your problems.

POWER UP!
In Real Life

Dear Mary

I liked your idea of asking a good question. I have five that I use to live the life I want.

1. **What have I done so far?** *I ask this to clarify whether or not I am in motion to help myself or to hinder myself. It is often the latter, if I am honest.*

2. **What is the worst that can happen?** *I am trying to give my fears a real shape with this one. Often an unshaped fear is greater than the reality that I later discover.*

3. **What would happen if I did nothing?** *This is an ownership question. Maybe I am taking on someone else's issues. Maybe the issues need to be resolved by others— and will be—if I don't intervene.*

4. **Whose help do I need?** *I don't need to be the Lone Ranger when facing tough times. Someone else has likely faced this, too, and will be happy to share their triumphs and defeats.*

5. **Finally, how does this fit with my bigger goals?** *I decided a few years ago to have some overarching "filters"*

through which I forced decisions to pass. Being post-fifty will do that. My colleague Steve Miller told me his big three are love, joy, and abundance. These are the goals that help him make daily decisions. I whisper those in my own ear as well and have decided for me that I will seek:

- *Intentional health*
- *Intentional joy*
- *Intentional gathering and sharing of useful knowledge*

I think we really are, in the long run, the sum total of:

- *The questions we ask*
- *The decisions we make*
- *The people with whom we have chosen to share our lives*

Thanks for asking.

Lou Heckler

A HOT FLASH OF POWER

Pose good questions. Ask the right ones and reap the rewards.

7

SHORE UP
Predict Your Achilles' Heel

Do you REMEMBER the story of Achilles? For those of you who cut Greek Mythology 101 class that day, Achilles was the bravest hero in the Trojan War. When Achilles was born, his mother, Thetis, tried to make him immortal by dipping him in the magic water of the Styx River. She held him by the heel, but as she immersed him, she forgot to dip him a second time so his heel could get wet too. (Somehow it's *always* the mother's fault.) As a result, the place on his heel where she held him remained untouched by the water of the Styx, and that part stayed mortal, and therefore vulnerable. Years later, he died in battle when an arrow pierced his heel. So to this day, we call a person's weak spot an *Achilles' heel.*

Everyone has an Achilles' heel. It's important to identify

it precisely because when we're feeling our most vulnerable, our urge to get a handle on life intensifies. We feel our sense of control slipping away and instinctively tighten our grip. The secret is to let go of our superwoman persona, recognize and accept what drives us into a frenzy, and then do everything we can to power up. In this manner, we can act in, believe in, and choose new ways that fill us with energy. We ultimately shorten our overwhelming list of what must be accomplished by preempting problems.

Here are Things to Think About as you explore the power of predicting your Achilles' heel.

Know Thyself

My Achilles' heel? I am overly sensitive to unkind criticism. That's not to say I am totally neurotic about it. I was born prematurely and have always suspected my nerves didn't cook long enough. I really appreciate feedback, even if it's severe. Some comments hit the mark and they make me say, as Julia Cameron wrote in *The Artist's Way,* "Aha! So that's what is wrong with it!" I'm coachable and can tolerate disappointment and overcome failure, but *please* don't criticize me with vague, malicious zingers. It's feels worse than getting a cold sore on my lip the night before the prom.

I remember a presentation I gave early in my career. I received wonderful evaluations and a standing ovation. But one (evil) woman wrote, "Mary seemed very self-impressed. She could have given that canned talk to an empty room." Ouch. That Trojan War arrow pierced my heel. I knew it was unwarranted, unkind, and untrue, but it hurt like the dickens. I suffered through a few of those remarks until I learned that I needed to acknowledge and, by doing so, protect my Achilles' heel. My initial strategy was to limit the number of times I used evaluations. I needed feedback but not from tens of thousands of people. One fellow speaker, however, told me she always used evaluation forms.

"Always?" I asked.

"Yes. Always."

I was surprised. "Wow. That's impressive."

She continued, "Oh, yes, I think it's very important to always receive written evaluations—and someday I hope to be strong enough to actually read them." Suddenly I felt much saner.

Second, I changed my belief system by developing a realistic expectation: Some people will like me, and others (poor misguided fools) won't. I wish they all liked me, but the truth is, many of them have their minds made up before I even open my mouth. It's true for all of us. Your "audience"—employees, committee members, supervisors, in-laws, neighbors—may like you just because they like you. Maybe you look like their favorite cousin Rosemary who as a child loved to play dress-up, or you sound just like their lovely Aunt Gertrude who always brought them dazzling birthday presents. They just simply like you.

They may also dislike you just because they do. You remind them of their cousin Rosemary who teased them unmercifully about their late-to-develop breasts, or you sound just like their Aunt Gertrude who remembered everyone's birthday but theirs. They don't like you the instant they meet you.

I concentrate on the ones who haven't decided yet.

Understanding my Achilles' heel allows me to distinguish between useful feedback and unkind criticism. I take the critiques and evaluate their merit. Often, if what someone says has a ring of truth to it, I will hear it from more than one person in ways that are frank but not unkind. I also know that when I feel that familiar pang in the gut, I can say, "Oh, there goes my Achilles' heel again. It's not a big deal; it's just my weak spot." I have learned that casting a light on my Achilles' heel makes it much less of a threat, and I'm more willing to let go.

> **Your weak spot need not cripple you. Identifying it allows you to lessen its grip on you as you lessen your grip on being perfect. What is your Achilles' heel?**

Keep It Above the Belt

The people we care about have an Achilles' heel too. To avoid alienating them we need to know what it is. Let's start with your husband or partner. Do you know what his or her Achilles' heel is? My husband's vulnerability is feeling stupid. He's a very bright guy, having taught for universities around the globe, so I was surprised to learn about this tender area. If I really want to escalate a fight and spend days saying I am sorry, then the best thing I can fire off in a heated debate is, "Well, if that isn't the stupidest thing I've ever heard!"

What about your partner? Do you know his or her sensitive spot? Is he embarrassed when you correct him in public? Does he feel rejected when you say no to sex? Does he develop a rash when you're overdrawn at the bank? Do you respect his shortcomings—or try to use them against him to obtain what you want? Your goal is to create a win-win outcome. Taking unfair advantage of others' weaknesses by hitting below the belt is a control technique. No one wins.

Kids have Achilles' heels too. My daughter Emily's weakness is boredom. She said to me, "Mom, I would rather have a bad experience than no experience." She really means it. Being bored is just about the worst punishment for her. This insight helps me be a much better mother, allowing me to let go when she gets restless.

My son Nicholas's weakness is disorganization—other people's. He likes routine, order, and timeliness, and I send him into orbit if I pick him up late or spring something on him at the last minute when he has his day already planned. When he was seven years old, he played T-ball. One 6:00 P.M. game was delayed for ninety minutes due to rain. In the third inning, at 8:00 P.M., I saw him walk out of center field, stop by the dugout for a moment, and head straight for the car. He had politely announced to the coach that it was his bedtime and he would have to go home now. The coach explained that the game was not over yet, but it made no impression on Nicholas. He was sorry about the rain delay, but it was time to go to bed.

I can't control Nick's Achilles' heel. I can encourage him

to be flexible. I can help him learn to delay gratification, and we can explore ways to keep his stress level down when chaos reigns. But in the meantime, we're all better off if I protect his soft spot. I arrive slightly early for carpool pick-ups and whenever possible let him know ahead of time if a schedule is changing. I am not trying to be his indentured servant. I'm just letting go of my need to control his quirks and tapping into my power by understanding what drives him nuts.

Knowing the Achilles' heel of others empowers you to interact more effectively and prevent problems. This principle hold true for your bosses, colleagues, in-laws, mother, and best friend. Do you know what their Achilles' heels are?

My dear grandmother's Achilles' heel was waste. Many of our elders grew up in the Great Depression or endured rationing through two world wars—experiences that had lasting effects on their views of money and consumption. I received this letter from my aunt, Sister Mary Ellen (Grandma's daughter), that explains how we can protect our loved ones' weak spots:

Dear Mary,

　　My mother believed in getting as much mileage from the clothes worn by her six children as she could. Living through the Depression and drought years on the farm, "I'll patch it" was a familiar phrase heard in our household. She spent hours in the evening patching different fabrics, and most often it was the knee area of the jeans worn by four brothers. Ecologically ahead of her time, she would cut the article into rag pieces when the material really warranted being disposed of.

My mother lived to the age of ninety-six. During the last active and independent years of her life, I had the privilege of living with and caring for her. I determined one Monday morning that my pajamas were worthy of disposal. I removed the buttons. (I had heard her say, "Never know when you might need a button.") This act always preceded the cloth's metamorphosis into a rag. I placed the garment in the wash and left for work.

Upon arriving home, I went to my room and changed into more comfortable clothes, and to my surprise, noticed my pajamas neatly folded on my bed with the buttons sewed on again. Enjoying the moment immensely, I mused that my mother observed my vow of poverty better than I did. When I laughingly broached the subject of the revitalized pajamas, she said, "There's nothing so worn about those pajamas that you can't wear them."

Now whenever I think about disposing of my "rags," I remember my mother's values and realize the riches of wisdom and practicality she has impressed upon me.

Sister Mary Ellen Schulte BVM

My grandmother was a very generous woman, but she never felt comfortable with excess, and there was no point in trying to change her. So Sister Mary Ellen wore the pajamas and honored her mother's sense of frugality. When Grandma's birthday rolled around, we always bought her a lovely gift she would never give herself like perfume, a hat for church, or a pretty handkerchief, but we were careful not to select something so extravagant that she would be uncomfortable using it.

Instead of recognizing and acclimating to a person's weak spot, many of us, unlike Sister Mary Ellen, often try to control it. We say, "I can change him! I can fix the problem, and everything will be better. I will ride in like a knightess in shining armor and save the day." I am reminded of the axiom, "A man gets married hoping his wife won't change. A woman gets married hoping he will." Sometimes we can make everything better by accepting the human foibles and adjusting our own approach. I remember overhearing my high school basketball coach, Bud McLearn, tell his assistant coach, "If you want Mary to do something, just tell her calmly. If you yell at her, she'll cry." It was true. While other girls really kicked their play up a notch when the coach scolded at full volume, my feelings got hurt. His astute insight into how to approach each player best accounts for one of the reasons he was inducted into the High School Girls Athletic Hall of Fame.

Bear in mind that protecting someone's weakness does not mean we should accept abuse, refuse to speak up for our rights, or become someone's slave. It means if their Achilles' heel is benign, protecting it may empower you both.

Being responsible for fixing the entire world and all the people in it can fill up a daytimer really fast and leave little time for the good life. Recognize others' soft spots, decide how you can best adapt, and let go of the need to repair all their broken parts.

Let Go of Pride

Some Achilles' heels are gender based. Many women have a bit of a, shall we say, navigation deficit. I'm not exaggerating when I say have no sense of direction whatsoever. Don't waste a first-class stamp mailing me a map. When I get the map in the mail, I smile. I look at the intersecting lines, the arrows, the little stars designating important landmarks, and the big star that says, "You are here." I think, "No, I'm not. I'm in the kitchen." The map might as well be carved on a grain of rice. I need directions that begin, "Open the garage door. Pull out of the driveway. Go in the direction of Jim and Darlene's house. (*Not* Kim and Christy's house. If you go past their house, you're going the wrong way.") My worst nightmare is when the direction giver speaks those dreaded words, "You can't miss it," because chances are I already have at least twice, and that's why I'm stopping again for more directions.

Verna, a seminar attendee in Hawaii, is one of millions of women who shares my affliction:

Dear Mary,

I need to drive a certain route to get to where I need to go. I will do it accurately only after driving the same route over and over again. If there is a detour for construction, it is all over. I have to start over from the beginning at home.

Frank and Ernest

SUPPORT GROUP FOR PEOPLE WITH NO SENSE OF DIRECTION - 1 MILE AGO

© 1996 Thaves / Reprinted with permission. Newspaper dist. by NEA, Inc.

My deficit is a serious Achilles' heel for someone who travels for a living, so it is important that I let go of pride. To cruise around the world successfully, I have to admit I need help, so I have established rules for the directionally impaired:

- *Never go anywhere new without explicit written directions.* By *written,* I do not mean scribbled abbreviations on a cocktail napkin. I don't let the direction giver use silly, vague terms like *north, south, right,* and *left.* I insist on specific instructions like, "Turn toward the blue gas station on the corner, and then go one block past the shopping mall."

- *Plan ahead.* I rely on good people to assist me. I call and make sure the drivers know where they are going because I will be of no help. I don't use false bravery. You will never hear me say, "I will meet you there." I say, "Can you wait for me?" (Translated, "Don't you dare leave without me!")

- *Be persistent.* When I ask for directions, I know I'll receive lots of misinformation. I'm not too proud to ask several people because one out of three of them is *totally* wrong. Others are less than helpful. By this, I mean that the instructions would confuse even Mensa members: they tell you to go up a "little hill," and when you arrive you find a 14,000-foot-steep mountain with Sherpas on the roadside.

- *Don't rent cars.* There's a better than fifty-fifty chance I will turn the wrong way out of the car rental parking lot and be two states over before I catch on.

I can honestly say I am almost never lost, though I do turn the wrong way coming out of the ladies' room at the movies. I've been known to leave a trail of bread crumbs (okay, potato chips) so I could retrace my steps. Still, I am not stupid. I just lack the gene that can decipher, "You are here."

Most of you are not anywhere near this pathetic. My sisters-in-law Kris and Sue are wonderful navigators, infinitely better map readers than their husbands. Still, if we give one hundred men and one hundred women a map and a destination, the men will have finished all the beer before most of us find the party. Research confirms that men are cognitively better equipped to handle spatial problems. CAT scans reveal that they use their left hippocampus, a little banana-shaped structure in their brain, to figure out where to go. Most women don't. Apparently, it would be better if we did. The gender gap on spatial skills is so wide that with 5 million students participating in the National Geography Bee, boys are forty-five times more likely to end up as finalists. It's doubtful I would even find the room where the bee was being held. I just figure nobody's perfect.

Maybe your Achilles' heel revolves around other gender-related issues. Do you frequently blame yourself for things that you aren't responsible for? Do you apologize when it's not your fault? Research shows that more women than men have these habits. We don't all share the same weaknesses, but as women we are predisposed to certain Achilles' heels.

> The gender gods deal both sexes some weak cards. Generally, and as much as we hate to admit it, we are genetically equipped or have been socialized to do some things better than others. So let go of pride; it's just a useless control technique. Admit your frailties and power up with your ABCs: Act. Believe. Choose. And *never* follow me.

Byte Me

Our society creates some Achilles' heels for us. Urban sprawl, with the resulting long commutes, traffic jams, and road rages, can drive many of us into the emergency room of life—figuratively and sometimes literally.

We also endure a lifestyle characterized by chronic interruptions. When I ask my audiences what they'd most like to control, they always mention interruptions. One woman told me she owns a consulting business and has an in-home office. She loved that she could keep an eye on the baby and the nanny and easily slip down to her office at odd hours to get some extra work done, which gave her more flexibility and time at home. Her inability to control the irritating interruptions, however, made her insane. Neighbors stopped by to chat, the deliverymen woke up the baby, and extra chores fell on her shoulders when her husband reasoned, "You're going to be home anyway."

Her highly effective female brain noticed everything that was going on around her. She felt overwhelmed with the responsibility of solving everyone's problems. Finally, she threw up her hands in defeat: "I feel as if I have to be in charge of it all, and I can't focus. I know my weakness: allowing chronic interruptions to disrupt my work. I also know my strength: I am the momentum gal. If I can get on a roll, I can really crank out the work and then go home, actually spending more time with my family. So I am renting an office nearby to keep my sanity."

Do I hear anyone say *technology?* When someone says *windows* in a word association game, do you answer *drapes?* Is *byte* something you hope your three year old stops doing at preschool? When your boss sends an e-mail informing you, "On Friday we're installing new company-wide software," do you secretly make little voodoo dolls in her image? You are not alone. Don't get the idea that everyone besides you is a perfectly competent computer genius. According to the Wirthlin Group, a Washington polling firm, nearly one in five VCR owners has failed one of the basic tests of the new information age: setting a digital clock. Eighty-eight percent of Americans own a VCR, and the number 12:00 is blinking endlessly on 16 percent of those machines. Although technology was designed to make our work easier, we have built a twenty-first-century Achilles' heel into our lives.

Perhaps your weak spot is just the opposite: you're a whiz kid with total dependence on technology. According to a 2000 *USA Today* digital dependency survey, 60 percent of respondents around the world say they can't live without their devices, and nearly four out of ten say the loss of their digital PC data "would be an unmitigated disaster." Mess with their computers, and they become high-tech wrecks.

If only we could get control over our ever-changing technology. Fat chance. It's time to power up with your ABCs. Identify your shortcoming. Too much technology? Not enough technocompetence? Then *act*. Take a class. Make friends with a computer guru in your office or the fourteen-year-old boy in your neighborhood. Get on a first-name basis with a computer doctor, just like you have a dentist and pediatrician. Get one that makes house calls and has an after-hours emergency number. Pick one night a week, and don't get on-line.

Believe that you are trainable to improve or reduce your interaction with a machine each day. You have experience with everything from training bras to training manuals, and you could probably write a best-seller called *Chicken Soup for the Toilet Trainer's Soul.* When home computers became mainstream, I held out for a while. I saw the users' vein-popping frustration and thought surely we would put ourselves out of our misery and go back to index cards. I've put that fantasy to rest and now focus on achieving a healthy balance of people and machines. *Choose* living over surfing. The efficiency of personal computers and all their digital cousins should create more time for the important things in life. Choose to be realistic. The washer and dryer quit. The refrigerator goes on the fritz. The car breaks down. Computers will too. (But isn't it weird that with a computer, when it freezes up you just turn it off and then back on again, and it mysteriously works just fine. That never happens with the vacuum cleaner after the kids have sucked up the bottle of spilled glue.)

Leslie Charles, author of *Why Is Everyone So Cranky?,* wrote, "Help me, I'm logged on and I can't get off!" Technology, traffic, chronic interruptions, and the other necessary evils created by our modern life will continue to be an Achilles' heel for many of us, as our world changes constantly and brings more bells and whistles that disconnect us. So power up! Examine your own life, and identify the factors in your day that drain your energy. Count how many minutes you talk in chat rooms, and compare that time to how many minutes you spend talking face to face with your partner. Could a one-day workshop spruce up your skills and reduce your technophobia? Should you reconsider carpooling to work? Who or what interrupts you the most? Is it time to set new boundaries?

When Helping Is Hurting

For most mothers, our children's pain is our greatest Achilles' heel. When our kids hurt, we ache even more. But our desire to prevent them from hurting often means that we try to control them, by either babying them—what psychologists call infantalizing—or making overly strict rules that even a warden wouldn't try to enforce. Years later, we may find we have actually impaired our children's emotional growth. The psychologist Charles Fay, of the Love and Logic Institute, said, "The kids who have the biggest problems in college are the ones who had overcontrolling parents or the ones who have parents who rescue them all the time. Neither set of kids knows how to make decisions, and they are coming to a time in their lives when things will get really hairy."

IN THE BLEACHERS   By Steve Moore

"Please go back to your seat, Mrs. Canfield. You don't see any of the other parents blocking for their kids, do you?"

We're responsible for keeping our children safe, *and* we're also responsible for teaching them age appropriate ways to keep *themselves* safe. We have to recognize that we're not going to like cutting the umbilical cord. We'll be tempted to bail them out of jams, solve their problems for them, and spare them from the logical consequences. This approach is perfectly reasonable and also the quickest way I know to handicap our kids. They must feel confident that they can solve their own problems by struggling and suc-ceeding. John and Linda Friel wrote in *The Seven Worst Things Parents Do,* "All parents would like to completely smooth the way for their children. Competent parents resist those urges because they know that over time, smoothing out all of life's rough edges will cripple their children and keep them from ever growing up. That is essentially the choice."

Giving in to our innate desire to protect and control our children also can prevent them from experiencing joy. I re-member the gift of self-esteem my father and mother gave my husband and me twenty-five years ago when we bought our first house. They said, "You know we can afford to help you, but we would not want to rob you of the thrill of buy-ing your home all by yourself." It certainly was a thrill. I know if economics dictated otherwise, they would have helped us get ahead in the world, but they were wise enough to recognize that the greatest gifts they could give us were self-sufficiency and self-respect.

If you're a parent, wanting to prevent your children's pain may always be your greatest weakness. Understand that, accept it, and use that knowledge so you don't let *your* Achilles' heel create an even bigger one for your kids. Acknowledge that you would crawl across a field of broken

glass to save them. Then, when the time is right, teach them the skills and offer them the love they need to figure out how to save themselves.

What About You?

Do you know what your Achilles' heel is? It may not be easy to confess that you're impatient, shy, procrastinating, chronically late, or testy when confronted. Who wants to admit to being a sitting duck for a salesperson's pitch and ending up with bills you can ill afford? Maybe you have a short fuse and say things you don't mean. Is it hard for you to say no to people who ask for your help? Debbie D'Amico, a manager for IBM, told me, "The very worst kind of Achilles' heel may be, in fact, not admitting you have one." Ignoring it is not going to make it go away. Leslie Charles wrote, "Sooner or later, whatever bugs us will come back and bite us in the backside if we do not take care of it up front. We never resolve what is hurting us so we never get a chance to heal from it. We distract ourselves by overscheduling, overworking and overspending, treating the symptoms instead of the cause. This constant state of combined denial and unrest can make us very cranky."

When we're stressed, that urge to control can get the best of us. If you get a leg up on your Achilles' heel and recognize those situations that tempt you most to control, you'll have a lot more energy each day.

TOOLS FOR YOUR REPAIR KIT
Shore Up!

1. Know your Achilles' heel in order to loosen its grip on you.

2. Predict and protect others' soft spots, and let go of the urge to fix them.

3. Let go of pride. Admit your frailties and ask for help.

4. Identify the factors in your world that drain your energy, and take microactions every day to counteract the negative forces.

5. Teach your children the skills, and offer them the love they need to figure out how to save themselves.

POWER UP!
In Real Life

Dear Mary,

I agree that everyone has an Achilles' heel. Over the course of my medical career, I have found that mine is sleep deprivation. We all know people who sleep six hours or even less and do just fine. I am definitely not one of them. I need eight full hours of sleep to function at my best—not six or seven or seven and one half, but eight hours. I can function for short periods on less, but I have learned not to push it. This fact comes in direct conflict with my job as a diagnostic radiologist. I am often called on to interpret films or perform procedures at all hours of the night and day. I also need to interact with patients, other physicians, and technologists during these times. Unfortunately, people get sick despite my personal biorhythm.

In my practice, every two months each member of the group takes call an average of one night per week and one weekend (Friday at 5:00 P.M. until Monday at 8:00 A.M., a stretch of 63 hours!). These weekend shifts finally did me in.

One weekend was particularly brutal. On Friday night, the emergency room kept me busy and awake most of the night. The following Saturday was a regular full workday at the hospital, plus I covered clinics in the area. Saturday night was worse than Friday. No sooner would I go to bed than I would have to get up, usually after I had just dozed off. The adrenaline

*would flow with each ring. By Sunday morning, I was just
about at my limit. Unfortunately, I still had twenty-four hours
to go. Sunday afternoon I got a call from one of my technologists asking for instructions for a radiology exam called a CAT
scan. It was a reasonable question really. The technologist was
very polite. Nevertheless, I became very angry. "Why are you
bothering me with a such simple question? What do the
doctor's orders say? Can't you figure this out on your own?" As I
was saying the words I knew I was being completely unfair, but
I could not stop myself. When I arrived at the hospital I continued to rant and rave until the tech finally put her hands on my
shoulders, shook me hard, and yelled, "Dr. Schulte, snap out of
it!" (To her credit, she is a very grounded person and knew I
was acting completely out of character.) I slithered away and
somehow made it through the weekend with no further inci-
dents.*

*After a full night's sleep, I felt terrible about my behavior
and vowed to do something about it. I knew the only way to
prevent a repeat performance was not to be in that situation
again. That meant I had to change the way I took call. As I
talked to my partners, many admitted that they too had had
similar experiences.*

*Now instead of weekend call, we have shift call. We divided
the weekends into twelve-hour days so we take call more frequently but for shorter periods of time. It turned out to be such
a good change that I no longer dread my weekend duties, and I
am actually fun to work with again. The changes were possible*

because I was willing, as you said, Mary, to predict what my Achilles' heel was and do something about it.

Sincerely,

William E. Schulte M.D.
President, Inland Imaging Diagnostic Radiology

A HOT FLASH OF POWER

Predict your Achilles' heel: You will turn your weakness into your strength and your failure into success.

8

WISE UP
Position Yourself

In LORNA LANDVICK's delightful novel *Patty Jane's House of Curl*, the main character quotes her mother's rather coarse but insightful advice: "Honey, life can be a ballroom dance or it can be full of shit. Your job in both cases is to watch where you step." What Patty Jane was referring to was the power we have to position ourselves strategically. Just like prime real estate, much of our influence hinges on location, location, location. But women are resistant to letting go and repositioning themselves. If we're responsible for every*thing*, then it follows we need to be every*where*. When I'm home, I think I should be at work. When I'm at work, I fret that I should be at home. My ambivalence is exhausting. Instead of trying to be everywhere, we should focus on spending time in the places that fill us with energy.

So how can we take Patty Jane's advice and step into the optimum positions and gain power? In this chapter you will learn how to get *to* bed, get *out* there, get *inside* their heads, get *away,* and get *off* a high horse.

So let's get on with it. Here are some Things to Think About as you consider the power of positioning.

Get to Bed

Unless you were raised by hyenas, you know that getting enough sleep every night is a key to good health. But do you know many women who actually sleep for eight hours every night? Me neither. Why not?

In the good old days, we could get a handle on many of our problems just by going to bed later and getting up earlier. That plan doesn't work so well anymore because there really is too much to do and not enough time to do it. We have not failed in some way. Our old strategy of stealing an hour or two from the Sandman to get a grip on our to-do list is now a joke. We could stay up all night, every night, and still not finish. Yet many of us haven't caught on. We wear our fatigue like a badge of honor. We settle for a lifetime of exhaustion and tell ourselves that crankiness, black circles under our eyes, and an aching body are the price we must pay to get it all done. After all, we remind ourselves, we are responsible for everything.

For many women, refusing to sleep is a control issue. We won't even let go long enough to close our eyes lest something get out of our jurisdiction. Take a nap? Why, that's a sign of not being needed. How will the earth continue to revolve on its axis if we take a break? Yes, I know that working, commuting, and especially caring for little children or our elders can legitimately take precedence over sleep. But be honest. Do you take advantage of the times they don't need you by getting enough sleep, or does snoozing rank near the bottom of your itinerary no matter what? Most of us decide that first we'll try to get everything done, and then we'll catch some sleep. No wonder we drop exhausted into bed too late each night.

So what can we do? For many women, robbing ourselves of sleep is a habit we wish we could break. We can get more of the respite we need if we ARM ourselves with power. It's a three-step approach: Accept, Respect, and Maximize:

Accept the fact that you won't get it all done. Sleep deprivation is not the answer to your "too-long-to-do list." It won't give you control. In fact, it sabotages us because it disconnects us from the energy we need to meet our ever-growing demands.

Respect yourself and your body enough to make sleep a priority. If scientists developed a pill that made us age slower, look prettier, lose weight, think and react faster, and feel more energetic and happier, there'd be riots in the streets outside the pharmacies as women clamored for it. We need to recognize a wonderful fact: we have found the fountain of youth, and it is called eight hours of uninterrupted sleep each night.

Maximize your chances of a good night's slumber. Yes, your kids will wake you up when they have a nightmare, and yes, occasionally your boss will request a last-minute report that's due in the morning. Sometimes your partner will become amorous on a night that you would trade your mother's heirlooms for some rest. I accept that a few of you might truly have only six free hours to doze, so make them the best six hours you've ever slept by creating a restful environment. The Better Sleep Council recommends:

- *Perform sleep rituals each night before you go to bed.* A lot of us race around 900 miles an hour all day and then slam on the brakes and expect to fall peacefully asleep immediately. Send your body signals that it's time to unwind with a nightly routine you enjoy: a hot bath, a good relaxing book (sorry, Stephen King), soft music, aromatherapy, or pampering skin care. You are not "just wasting time." You need to prepare to sleep.

- *Avoid alcohol and strenuous exercise too close to bedtime.* These don't make you tired and promote sleep. They interfere with your natural rhythms.

- *Sleep in a cool, quiet, dark room.* Your ever-vigilant female brain responds to light and noise. Use white-noise tapes or ear plugs, or get some of those sexy eye shades and feel like a movie star.

- *Make sure your mattress is comfortable and big enough.* You spend a third of your life in bed. Make it an oasis.

I know sometimes it's hard to let go and say good night so allow me to give you some incentive to sleep more. A research study published in the *Journal of the American Medical Association* (August 2000) reports that middle-aged weight gain may be due to a lack of slow-wave (deep) sleep. As people age, they tend to get less slow-wave sleep, which can cause a decrease in growth hormone. Certain kinds of weight gain are associated with growth hormone deficiencies. In addition, research published in the December 2000 issue of the journal *Nature Neuroscience* suggests that a good night's sleep is necessary for the brain to store the memory of what has been learned during the day. *Translation for the sleep-deprived woman:* Get enough sleep, and you could wake up smarter, and with a flatter stomach and thinner thighs. What are you waiting for? Position yourself prone, and get to bed!

> **Sleep deprivation is often a control technique that backfires. Remind yourself: Sleep is not optional. Give yourself permission to go to bed.**

Get Out There!

Harry Beckwith wrote in *Selling the Invisible,* "Let opportunity hit you." He was referring to marketing strategies, but the principle holds true for life. I call this kind of positioning "standing in the traffic." Standing in the traffic means you will have to risk and experiment a little. Sure you might get hit, brushed back, or maimed. It might even kill you (or your dreams.) On the other hand, someone just might pull over to the side of the road and yell, "For goodness sakes, get in. I can see you need a ride, and I happen to be going there myself. I'll show you the way." Amazingly wonderful things can happen when you open yourself up to the possibilities and then just gently put yourself out there in the middle of it.

The first step is to shake things up in your life. One of the cards in Roger von Oech's *Creative Whack Pack* (dubbed "a creative thinking workshop in a box") reads, "The more often you do something in the same way, the more difficult it is to think about doing it in any other way. Break out of this 'prison of familiarity' by disrupting your habitual thought patterns." So ride your bike to work, eat potato chips with your nondominant hand, wear purple socks with your navy suit, or write a love poem in the bathtub. Shaking things up can lead to new ideas, and new ideas can bring you power.

MAIL SOMEONE SOMETHING

There's something magical about the mail. Sending a letter must emit all sorts of vibrations because an incredible chain of events can occur even years later. Letters sent to servicemen during Operation Dear Abby (a letter-writing campaign to thank our armed services personnel for their dedication), result in many marriages. Relatives forgive longstanding grudges just by getting a single note of apology. Long-lost lovers have reunited fifty years later because of a three-line postcard.

I too discovered a bit of magic when I sent a letter in 1993 to Jonellen Heckler, author of *Circumstances Unknown.* I wrote to her because I do not (repeat, do *not*) read murder mysteries; I am scared enough in my daily life as it is. I like novels where boy meets girl, they're separated, and their love brings them back together. Then they sing and dance and get married in the end. (Okay, not quite that sappy but close.)

Still, several people raved about Jonellen's book so I read one page (a microaction). I knew I would dislike it and could quit. Instead, I was immediately and helplessly hooked and even lingered over the last few pages, not wanting it to end. I wrote a letter to Jonellen to tell her how much I enjoyed her work:

September 15, 1993

Dear Jonellen,

Wow! Can you write! I read Circumstances Unknown *this summer on vacation. Although I admire your immense talent, I felt compelled to write to the new surgeon general with some recommendations regarding your work. I have enclosed a copy for you. Keep up the writing. I can't wait until your next book.*

Sincerely,

Mary LoVerde

In a feeble attempt to be clever, I also wrote a mock letter on the university letterhead (where I was working at the time) to the new surgeon general of the United States:

September 15, 1993

Joycelyn Elders, M.D.
Office of the Surgeon General
Washington, D.C.

Dear Dr. Elders,

Congratulations on your recent appointment to Surgeon General. It sounds like those confirmation hearings are something else.

I know you will be pretty busy with AIDS, teenage pregnancy, suicide, and cardiovascular disease, but I wanted to call your attention to a powerful new product on the market that could have major health implications. I took the liberty of suggesting some "Surgeon General warnings." I recently read Circumstances Unknown *by Jonellen Heckler. I recommend the book come with the following warning:*

> **Surgeon General warning: This product may cause sleep deprivation (because you won't be able to put it down).**

Then my husband read it.

Surgeon General warning: This book may cause you to neglect your spouse and children (because you won't be able to put it down).

Over the following weeks I read her other novels, A Fragile Peace *and* Safekeeping.

Surgeon General warning: This book may be habit forming. It never causes drowsiness. Easily excitable persons should check with their doctor first.

Thanks for considering my suggestions. If you need any help with the health care reform bill, tell Hillary to give me a call. I've got lots of ideas.

Sincerely,

Mary LoVerde, M.S., A.N.P.
Director of Hypertension Research Center

Unfortunately, I did not know that my secretary did not know that *this was a joke.* So you can imagine my surprise when I got a letter back from the surgeon general of the United States on her letterhead:

Dear Ms. LoVerde:

> *I was moved by your kind letter of support, and will do everything in my power to stay focused, to speak clearly, and to do my part in leading all of us in nurturing our precious resource—our children.*
>
> *I intend to reread your letter whenever I feel the obstacles are too great. As I said during my confirmation, I'm happy to be the lightning rod if there is thunder behind me. Thank you for being that thunder.*

Sincerely,

M. Jocelyn Elders, M.D.
Surgeon General, U.S.P.H.S.

I am obviously fortunate that Dr. Elders does not actually read her mail. I'm sure her staff had a hard time figuring out which form letter to send to the crazy woman in Colorado.

Although I felt ridiculous, I thought I should confess to the author in case the FBI called her to investigate. Luckily, Jonellen has a great sense of humor and a soft spot in her heart for fools. We became friends.

BUT THAT'S NOT ALL

I also got acquainted with Jonellen's husband, Lou, a famous keynote speaker. One of the lines in his speech had a profound effect on me. I wrote the line on a card and put it in my closet where I could see it daily. I read that card every day, sometimes several times a day. Five years later, when I wrote my first book, Lou generously allowed me to use his line as the opening quotation of Chapter One.

My editor disliked the title I had selected for my book, so when I sent the final manuscript in, I left off the title page entirely, thinking to myself, why aggravate her with something she has already vetoed? Lou's quote was now at the top of the first page of the manuscript. A few days later, my agent called me and raved, "Simon & Schuster just *loves* your new title!"

I was confused. "No kidding? What is it?"

She said, "*Stop Screaming at the Microwave!*"

Without a first page, my editor thought Lou's opening quote in Chapter One was the new title! The book's title has opened many doors for me, and more important, both Lou and Jonellen have become dear friends and profound influences in my professional life.

I sent out one letter, and my position in the world changed dramatically.

There is no way I could have planned for, guided, or controlled these events. I could not have foreseen that mailing the letter would give me the title for my book or bring two fabulous people into my life. I did have to *act:* I wrote the letter. I did have to *believe:* I knew that connecting with someone brings joy. I did have to *choose:* I took a risk and actually mailed the letter.

Richard Armour's poem cleverly describes the power of positioning.

> *Shake and shake*
> *The catsup bottle.*
> *None will come*
> *And then a lot'll.*

The good things in life are often like that catsup bottle. Power is energy, and energy is vibration. Use your power to shake things up. Send an e-mail. Take up archery. Get a part-time job at the hardware store. Stand in the traffic.

Get Inside Their Heads

The concept of positioning works as a valuable parenting tool. You will be tempted in all sorts of ways to coerce your kids to comply. Try not to. Part of their developmental task is to resist and become autonomous, so by forcing, you're just playing into their hands. Yes, there will be times when you need to scoop your two year old off the grocery store floor because she is in the middle of a temper tantrum. You will reposition her in the car seat and drive home exhausted and frustrated. Goading her to cheer up will fail. Remember how well the phrase, "Stop crying or I will give you something to cry about," worked when you were growing up? Instead of mentally strong-arming the kids, take a tip from the Godfather and "make 'em an offer they can't refuse."

Colleen Weil, a nurse from Shelton, Washington, told me how difficult mornings were at her house. She had to be at the hospital at 7:00 A.M., which meant getting her three small boys up at 4:30 A.M. every day and driving them to their day care home. Winter mornings made it especially hard to lure the boys out of their warm waterbeds to get dressed. She said that after months of pleading, threatening, and repeated trips to their bedrooms, which often made her late for work, she stopped prodding them and tried another tactic. Five minutes before it was time for the boys to get up, she put the clothes they had laid out for the day into the dryer. Then she brought the toasty clothes to them and said gently, "Time to get up. Hurry now and get dressed while your clothes are nice and warm." Problem solved. No more threats. No "or elses." She changed her position, so they could change theirs. She looked at the situation from their point of view and powered up by figuring out how it could be to their benefit to get up on time. What ingenuity!

Rethink your position of forcing your kids. Stand at a slightly different angle, and outsmart them instead.

Get Away

Some of us feel so responsible for everything that we decline to go on vacation. According to a 2001 Work and Family Institute survey, 25 percent of workers do not take all their vacation each year. For others, we might leave work, but our minds are so busy we don't really get away. I recently read a study that found that 64 percent of managers take their laptops with them on vacation. I believe the data. I've seen some of these people with their computers at the beach.

Everyone needs a vacation. In a world that demands better, more, faster, and sooner, reenergizing by going on vacation is mandatory. Study after study shows the decline in productivity and increase in errors and injuries when we refuse to take a break. Other research reveals that people who do not take a vacation regularly may be more likely to have a heart attack or even die from it than those who do vacation regularly.

Once again, let's remind ourselves: There is too much to do. We could work 24/7 and still not get everything done. Rationalizing away the need for downtime is a control technique that saps us of energy in the long run.

Some women tell me that going away is so much trouble they'd just rather stay home. I know what they're talking about because I used to believe that too. Before I left on vacation, I'd feel compelled to edge the yard, polish the silver, clean my closet, and scrub the entryway tile grout with a toothbrush. I'd make a list of instructions for the babysitter that was so involved it could earn her twelve college credits toward becoming an nuclear physicist. Then I'd get up at 5:00 A.M. to clean all the windows, sort the spools of thread in my sewing basket by color, and back out of the house vacuuming.

Yes, I know we like to unplug the iron and tidy things up so the house is a nice place to come home to. But in my exhausted grouchy state, it's no wonder I thought vacations were "work." I made them a grind with my refusal to let go of my perfectionism.

So I have changed. I no longer make 400 frozen meals before I leave "so I won't have to cook when I get home." I have also focused on making sure I am really present during my time off. My family goes to the lake each summer, and I create an electronic-free zone for two weeks. I totally abstain from any phone, fax, e-mail, Web site, or pager for fourteen days. The first year I followed this, I was sure the planets would fall out of their orbit if I was not on-line, but Saturn, Pluto, and the others carried on quite nicely without me. The next year, I was convinced my clients would bail out on me if I failed to return their calls immediately, but my assistant handled things beautifully; the majority of my customers waited patiently until I got back, and many were inspired to take a little break themselves. Now I look forward to the time away from the electronic tethers, and I am comfortable with the fact that, hard as it is to believe, the world can limp along for a couple of weeks without my help.

I can't begin to describe the sense of freedom and power I feel by the end of my vacation. Maybe that's because the word *vacation* comes from the Latin word, *vacans,* meaning "to vacate" or "to be empty." Jamming our lives with responsibilities 365 days a year causes a blockage. We open the clog by creating a void. So get empty, and see if that vacuum allows energy to flow to you.

"I MISS MY MOMMY"

A getaway with your partner or best friend should be at least an annual event. I fully acknowledge that it's often hard to leave the kids behind and take some time for personal relationships. You know you will miss your children, and of course, they'll miss you too, but, really, left in the loving care of relatives or friends, they'll be just fine. The writer Nora Ephron quipped that it is perfectly reasonable for your children, given the choice of having their mother either enjoy herself in Hawaii or sit in the next room contemplating suicide, to pick "in the next room" just about every time. So don't stay home just because your kids prefer it. You need to get away. Here is a tip that you might adapt to ease the separation anxiety for both you and the kids.

One year when I vacationed with my husband, I learned from the babysitter that the toughest time for our kids, then ages two, five, and eight, was bedtime. Fatigue made for fragile feelings, and they cried, "I want my mommy!" So before the next trip, I wrote each child a letter for each day I was gone, labeling it, "Open on Monday," "Open on Tuesday," and on through the week. I wrote about the things I knew they would be doing that day. At the end of the letter, I would send them on a little hunt. I instructed them to go look under the sofa, or in the bottom of the laundry basket, and at each location they'd find another note. I reminded them of something I admired about them or recalled a fond memory. The kids opened the notes just before bedtime and then traipsed upstairs and down, following the trail of hidden notes. The final note was attached to a little toy, book, or a small treat I knew they'd enjoy. The day before I came home, the last line read, "The best gift of all is my love for you. I'll be home in the morning!"

The babysitter said the kids got so excited about the "adventure," as they came to call it, that they begged to go to bed earlier and earlier as the week progressed. Though arranging the hunt meant spending some time before I left, I loved knowing that I didn't have to spend my relaxation time shopping for overpriced trinkets. Most important, we all went to bed remembering how much we love each other. The little game allowed each us to let go a little easier.

One woman said to me, "Get real! Do you have a personal valet? How do you have enough time to write all those notes? I can hardly find time to buy milk before I leave!" I hear her. The point isn't that we make elaborate games before we take off. The point is, What can you do so that you stop feeling guilty about leaving? You deserve to get away. For me, I had to find a way to stop my kids' nighttime tears so I could relax and have fun. What is your barrier to leaving? How could you remove it?

ARE WE HOME YET?

When we take a family trip, we also have to be alert to our desire to get a handle on everything on the way back from vacation. Traveling home never seems to be as much fun as it was to travel there. Family members may be cranky, and the little personality quirks that started out being fun make you want to pull out your eyelashes. The kids are throwing things out the windows, which the flight attendants frown on, and there is an unidentified odor emanating from your three year old's suitcase.

Your first reaction may be to tense up and threaten, "Everyone should simmer down, or we won't pull over at the next rest stop." That plan will most likely backfire on you. Instead, redirect their energy into playing "Best." The whole family will enjoy it. The Best game is played by asking everyone to take a turn at describing what they consider the best in each category. Best meal on the trip. Best activity. Best laugh. Best person they met. Best hotel. Best swimming pool. Best day. Best purchase. Best new thing they learned, and finally, best of the best. Then to help them begin reentry into life at home, I always ask, "What is the best thing about going home?"

Not only does this game distract your clan from putting beans up each other's noses (and you've asked your husband very nicely on several occasions not to do that), you'll learn things you didn't know about your family when you play this game. You might find out they liked seeing the shooting star as they sat around the campfire better than shooting at the video arcade that cost you forty-eight quarters, that the best "person" they met was the scrawny stray dog you let them feed the rest of their burger to, and that the best thing about going home was eating in their own kitchen instead of a fast-food restaurant.

Linda Coughlin tried this game on the way home from a frustrating camping trip with her three school-aged children. Her family had just bought a camper, and neither she nor her husband was proficient at backing up the car with it attached, so stopping to eat or get gas usually meant one of them threatened to file for divorce. On the way up the mountain, ten-year-old Brandon got carsick and they had to stop every five miles to change his clothes and put the soiled ones in a bag. By the time they got to the top of the pass, Brandon had worn his entire suitcase full of clothes, and they had been gone only two hours. They stopped at a little laundromat so Linda could wash and dry the clothes. Being the good mom that she is, she spread a blanket on the folding table and took out the sandwiches she'd brought along, and they had a picnic right there in the laundromat. An hour later, they were on their way and had a grand time for the next week. And yes, you guessed it, on the way home, all three children voted the best of the best was the picnic in the laundromat. What Linda thought was the low point of the vacation was the actually the apex.

The Best game is also a wonderful exercise at work, at the end of projects, or as a closing exercise for committees. We can't make people relax and have a good time, but we can put them in the best frame of mind and up the odds.

> Get away on vacation, and fill up with energy. Write in a journal about the places you'd like to tour. Buy a tent. Visit travel Web sites, and investigate discounted airfares and hotels. Start grooming a college student so she or he can babysit for the weekend. Make a list of the reasons that you can't go on vacation, and start crossing them off. Life is short. Let go.

Get Off Our High Horses

Humans usually resist change and make all kinds of excuses to avoid it. "It will never work." "We tried that before and it failed." "If we make that move, it will ruin everything we've worked for so far." Instead of pooh-poohing each new idea, consider repositioning your position.

When the concept of renting home videos first came out, resistance was fierce. The naysayers cried, "Why, the movie industry will go the way of eight-track stereos when CDs hit the market. Who will go to the movie theater and pay seven dollars if you can rent it a few months later for two dollars?" Apparently, millions of people will, and then they will spend billions more dollars renting the movies they missed or want to see again.

When the government proposed increasing the speed limit from 55 to 75 miles per hour on some highways, I, and many of my fellow Americans, predicted carnage on the interstate. "What could these morons be thinking? I don't care if the engineers are convinced the highways are designed to carry people safely at higher speeds. They're crazy!" It turns out they were sane, and I and my gang of Highway Hellions were wrong. Highway deaths went down 11 percent, probably in part due to seat-belt laws and aggressive police crackdown on road rage. Nevertheless, the predicted doom and gloom never materialized.

Most of us can recall countless examples like these. We do things the same way, even when those things don't work very well, because we like the sense of control that repetition gives us. We might be miserable, but we're predictably miserable. Unfortunately, when we do that, we sometimes stifle good ideas.

Power up by opening your mind to the possibilities; then reposition your thinking. Narrowing our positions can narrow our options. Surrendering to change might lead

you to newness and excitement. What changes are you willing to consider?

Making a Choice

These examples demonstrate how we can power up. If we are willing to let go and get enough sleep each night and also regularly leave our troubles behind and get away on vacation, energy will flow to us. If we are open and flexible and agree to change our point of view so we can see another's position and if we release our need to know all the answers, knowledge will come easily. If we are brave enough to stand in the traffic and let opportunity hit us, and then be confident and positive enough to shake things up, our wildest dreams may come true. It's our choice.

TOOLS FOR YOUR REPAIR KIT
Wise Up!

1. **ARM** Yourself with Power
   - *Accept* the fact you won't get it all done, and give yourself permission to go to bed.
   - *Respect* yourself and your body enough to make sleep a priority. Drink from the fountain of youth: Sleep!

- **Maximize** your chances of a good night's slumber by creating an environment conducive to rest.

2. Stand in the traffic and shake things up.

3. Position yourself at a slightly different angle, and outsmart your kids.

4. Unplug and go away on vacation.

5. Play the Best game

6. Open your mind to the possibilities.

POWER UP!
In Real Life

Dear Mary,

As an assignment during class, we were asked to do five things differently to make a change and "shake things up" a little. I wrote a few ideas down before I left class, but as I was driving home, I came up with different ideas.

I don't usually eat breakfast with my family at home. I

make breakfast, but I am usually out the door in the morning without eating, so I decided that one of my changes would be to make breakfast for dinner. I prepared pancakes, scrambled eggs, bacon, sausage, and rice. I set everything out on the table. Needless to say, they were surprised and really enjoyed it. So we were all able to sit down and have "breakfast" for dinner.

The next day, I found out the boys told their friends about the breakfast, and their friends thought that was cool! My sons told me their friends said, "My mom doesn't do anything fun like that!" Now I was the surprised one because they want to do this once a month.

Jodi Chang
Wahiawa, Hawaii

A HOT FLASH OF POWER

Position yourself. Place your mind, body, and soul in the best possible position to receive all the abundance the universe has to offer.

9

PAIR UP
Partner with Women

WHEN ANOTHER WOMAN offers her help, do you some-times think, "Oh, no. I wouldn't want to impose," or "Gee, thanks, but it will be easier to do it myself"? Some of us think that asking for help is a sign of weakness. If we are really strong, capable women, shouldn't we be able to han-dle our lives on our own? Actually, the opposite is true. We can gain tremendous power by partnering with other women.

On one hand, our natural tendency is to work together. Unlike the male pyramid structure, where one man is at the top and competition and winning are paramount, in the flat female hierarchy, we see ourselves as equals and seek con-nections and make decisions by generating consensus among peers. We're especially good at helping women who fall below the line. We pride ourselves on rallying around and bringing her back up to our level. When we get just a glimpse of crisis—divorce, trouble with kids, money woes, depression—we circle around with the correct dose of healing medicine.

On the other hand, we're generally not as good at boosting women up to the next level or even watching them use their own power to rise above. We wonder if their success detracts from our own. We're often a lot more comfortable if the playing field remains flat because it keeps our jealousies and insecurities in check. How often when we hear of someone's good fortune do we think, "Well, it sure must be nice to have great legs [or an attentive husband, a telecommuting job, or help at home]." Our quip may be said in jest, but there is an underlying scolding: "How dare you rise to another level!" Some women find a way to grab her by the hem of her skirt and bring her back to "where she belongs."

Many other factors play a role in our failure to partner successfully with one another. We're often accused of getting our feelings hurt too easily, which leads to unnecessary conflicts, and of having trouble separating business decisions from personal emotions. Mark George, of the National Institute of Mental Health, scanned the brains of ten men and ten women while they were recalling sad events. The women' brains were eight times more active than the men's, supporting other research studies suggesting that women may experience feelings more profoundly than men do. We can appear to be overly sensitive.

Okay, we have our faults. So sue us. The point is we *need* each other, even though we may run into conflict. We hunger for supportive bonds, but our predilection to handle things all by ourselves gets in our way and drains us of energy. It's time to renew our focus on one of our most significant powers: pairing up with other women.

Here are Things to Think About as you ponder your power to partner with women.

Form an Alliance

Each year my best friend, Brenda, and I meet at a destination spa for four days of renewal. The last night after dinner, we announce to each other what we will let go of, that is, what aspect of our lives we will be "leaving" at the spa. We identify one fear, belief, or action that is blocking our energy and interfering with our power. We commit to helping each other with our pledge when we get back home.

This year I gave up my fear of aging. It's not that I am all that old, but little signs that I'm not getting any younger keep cropping up. I went to bed one night with perfect vision, and the next morning when I got in my car, I had to get into the back seat to read the odometer. I drove to the drug-store and bought a dozen pairs of reading glasses. I have them in every room in the house because I just can't make myself wear them on a chain around my neck.

I work out regularly to fight off the effects of gravity. At forty-eight, I understand that nothing sags up, and I fear the day when gravity wins. Although I realize I should be grateful to be alive, I am ever so slightly concerned about more gray hair, a thickening middle, and the growing crescendo of creaking joints. Wrinkles bother me. I know I can't control them, though I did sign up for the anti-aging facial at the spa this year. The aesthetician took one look at me and had the audacity to suggest the *ultimate* anti-aging facial for only fifty dollars more. As I said, I have noticed subtle signs.

When I turned forty, I got two terrific cards that I have never forgotten. One said, "You're forty." And inside it read, "Kind of makes that little depression you had when you were thirty seem sort of silly, doesn't it?" What a great phi-losophy. If I am lucky enough to make it to some more of those birthdays with a zero in them, I hope I feel the same. I suspect ten years from now I am going to think I looked like "da bomb" at forty-eight.

The other birthday card said something like, "In your twenties you worry about what everyone is thinking about you. In your thirties you don't worry so much about what everyone is thinking about you. And in your forties, you realize, *no one* was thinking about you!" It's true. Most people are much more concerned with their own lives than anything you have going on in yours.

As we age, some of our neuroses fade. I used to beat myself up for days after I made a mistake. Now I realize that at the exact moment I am reliving my error, I am the only one on the planet obsessing about it. Everyone else has moved on. So if they are no longer focusing on it, why should I? As I age, I am smarter, more relaxed and confident, and not nearly as dependent on outsiders for approval. I'm coming to understand that at any age I can still enjoy the great joys of life: kids, lovemaking, chocolate, friends, my cat, gardens, evening walks, and perfect-fitting jeans 50 percent off. No matter how old I get, I imagine people will still turn me on, books and movies will make me laugh and cry, and beauty will move me deeply. So I will exercise, eat a healthy diet, dye my hair, and pay way too much for wrinkle cream. I'll lie to my friends about how young they look if they promise to lie to me. I'll wear funny little bifocals so I can see. My friend Christy suggested I buy leopard-print glasses and a really funky chain and get over it. I like her advice.

I will, I hope, grow old. To remind myself of my commitment, I've placed a line from the poem "Desiderata" on my desk: "Gracefully surrender the things of youth." There's that *surrender* word again.

At the spa, Brenda and I reasoned all this out over a glass of wine. I left my fear back there, and I feel more powerful because I have a friend who understands and will help me when the fear reappears.

Many women have told me about their success with forming a female alliance like this. One asked her friend to help her simplify by reducing her clutter, which included an old shirt she'd been making for a former boyfriend—and she's been married fifteen years! Another woman said she paired up with her friend and powered up to let go of her need to please her mother by keeping an immaculate house. When her mother comes to visit, she calls her ally for a "re-minder" pep talk.

> **It's easier to give up our desire to control the uncontrollables of life when we merge our energy with another woman. What do you need to let go of, and who could you pair up with to help you?**

Defend Each Other

When I was twenty-eight years old, I attended a fashion show emceed by a female celebrity who had launched a new line of clothes. It was the most clever show I've ever attended because each model entered the runway looking rather plain, and then with just a few changes—as the addition of scarves, belts, shoulder pads, jewelry, hats, and different shoes or jacket—mediocre turned into Madison Avenue chic. The sixty-plus-year-old celebrity asked one model to make certain wardrobe changes onstage. The young woman didn't understand the instructions and became a bit flustered as she tried to comply. The emcee kept telling her again and again, in an increasingly condescending tone. The model finally made the correct alterations, and the older woman turned to the audience and said, "I'm sorry, but God made her *pretty*." Embarrassed, the model fled the stage.

Twenty years later, I still deeply regret that I sat there in silence. Why didn't I stand up for this young woman and tell the celebrity that if this was the kind of "beauty" she was selling, I wasn't interested? Watching a woman publicly humiliate another made me feel ugly. Oh, how I wish I could go back to that day.

We have many opportunities to speak up now to defend other women. For example, what was the matter with us when we watched Katherine Harris, the state attorney general of Florida, get ripped when she was thrown into the spotlight because of voting irregularities in the 2000 presidential election? I'm not talking about her legal opinions. Never mind our political leanings or our diverse positions on pregnant chads and statewide recounts. Criticize her politics; it's the American way. But the press and the comedians made fun of her clothes, hair, and makeup. What does her appearance have to do with her decisions on voting laws? I'm not naive; I know political forces on both sides try to vilify people to discredit them. But why are we putting up with it? Why wasn't every woman in America having a fit and making her views known?

When we see women being unfairly attacked, we're often reluctant to defend one another. There are many reasons; insecurity, jealousy, fear, feelings of powerlessness. Still, we are making a big mistake when we fail to speak up, because one day it may be our turn to sit on the hot seat. Who will defend us?

When we join forces with other women, our power grows exponentially. Natalie Angier wrote, "I want to discover anew the value of sisterhood, of females sticking up for each other, which the bonobos [pygmy chimpanzees] do to such a degree that they are rarely violated or even pestered by males, despite the males being larger and stronger." Natalie's words inspired me. I figure if tiny chimps can stand united, so can we. Therefore, I have made it a personal policy never to sit idly by when I see a woman being hurt. I can choose to speak up, write letters, make calls, send money, or work to change laws, but I will no longer be silent.

I heard Dr. Maya Angelou discuss how she handles this

issue: "Having courage is the greatest virtue. You can be courageous in small ways." Her policy? "I don't stay in a room where racial pejoratives are being thrown about. I don't stay in a room if there is female bashing going on. I say, 'Gosh it's eight o'clock. I'm supposed to be in Bangkok.' And I leave the room." Walking out is her simple but powerful microaction in defense of women.

> **Dr. Angelou reminds us that our values are demonstrated by what we will not tolerate. What's your policy in situations like these? Have you ever defended a woman in her time of need? Do you have any regrets for failing to do so? Have you thanked a woman for standing up for you? Defend each other. Women need other women.**

Combat Destructive Behavior

Not only do we fail to defend each other, we sometimes outright sabotage one another. That was a hard sentence for me to write, but it's true. Can you think of a time another woman sabotaged you at work? I asked the association president of a female-dominated industry why there were so few young women in the field, and she replied, "We tend to eat our young." Dr. Judith Briles, author of *Women to Women 2000: Becoming Sabotage Savvy in the New Millennium,* reports that the problem of female sabotage in the workplace has become 45 percent more frequent than when she first studied it over twenty years ago. Her findings reveal that unlike men's direct style of confrontation, women often sabotage other women in a covert and indirect manner. Her research indicates that in many instances, women who sabotage appear to do so to stay in control.

In 1983, I gave birth to our second child. Ten days later, baby Emily and I flew across the country for three days of medical research training. Insane, I agree, but it was the era of superwomanhood, and I had a long list of reasons that I had to go: I was the only qualified researcher for the training, there was a $350,000 grant attached, and so on. My male corporate client was very gracious and even made a tiny official name tag for Emily.

When I returned home, I (very reluctantly) had to go back to my clinic to begin the research study. Emily came with me to work each day and slept and played in a crib in my office. She almost never cried. I didn't ask anyone for assistance, and for the most part, we stayed out of sight. My male boss was happy with my willingness to come to work at all and was in full support of my decision to bring Emily. The patients looked forward to their visits with the "cute little researcher." We perked along nicely for about four months, but as Emily grew, I knew she needed more stimulation and space than I could provide in my office. Though I hated to leave her, I arranged for in-home child care. The next day, I had a visit from a clinical supervisor who managed the women working in the offices around me. She admitted that, behind my back, they had held meetings complaining that I was bringing my baby to work. The women identified no specific concerns such as noise, patient complaints, or office disruption of any kind; they just thought it was "wrong." I felt betrayed. The women were all either single and childless or their children were grown and "they certainly hadn't been allowed to bring their babies to work." I was so taken aback that all I could do was mumble that I had already arranged for child care and Emily would no longer be a "problem." They did exactly what Dr. Briles described: sabotaging me with covert and indirect tactics.

Three years later, that same supervisor had a baby. When she returned from her maternity leave, she came into my office and with tears in her eyes said, "I am sorry for ever complaining that you brought your ten-day-old baby to work. I was childless then and absolutely clueless to the sacrifices you were making. I left my six-week-old baby to come to work today and cried all the way here. I am so sorry I hurt you." I was grateful for her honesty and will always remember her grace and humility.

Some women are vindictive, vengeful types who plot

to destroy you. Others sabotage but rationalize their actions by blaming peer pressure and politics. Sabotage is a self-defeating behavior for women. It is in direct conflict with a philosophy of being kind as a way of life. In addition, we never know when we might need help, or be in a similar situation.

> Women can be their own worst enemies, but we also have the power to be our most ardent supporters. Become sabotage savvy. Move from sabotage to support by identifying and understanding the backstabbing behaviors of others, having the courage to confront the saboteur, and making a commitment to honor other women. Your first microaction is to pair up.

Ease Your Territorial Tendencies

Women are territorial beings, which often makes it hard to share: she took my idea; she stole my boyfriend; she got my promotion; she wore my dress to the party. I got a message loud and clear this year to reexamine my own territorial tendencies and consider the power of partnering. My lesson came in two parts. First, in 1997, author Kay Allenbaugh published one of my stories in her national bestseller, *Chocolate for a Woman's Soul*. The story, called the

"Tootsie Roll Ritual," relates the tale of how my grandfather always gave me Tootsie Rolls when I came to visit. I was honored to have my work included in her book.

Four years later, I got the following fax from Kay Allenbaugh:

Dear Mary,

I received the most amazing story from Merilee Glick yesterday. Feel free to use it in your talks if you'd like. I guess I shouldn't be surprised by now at how God works. The world just keeps getting smaller and smaller as we intertwine in each other's lives. Much love and gratitude for all you do in the world,

Kay

Here's the story she sent me:

Born six years, eleven months and twenty-six days after me, Nancy, my sister, always seemed to be at a different place in her life than I was. She played with dolls while I started dating. Then I got married and had babies as she started dating. When she had a family, I returned to the work force. As I passed fifty and she was approaching forty-five we were finding similar interests and becoming good friends. As I was packing for a month of studying Spanish and having fun in Costa Rica, Nancy was packing for a week in Austria with her husband, David, to be followed by two weeks with their family and some friends on a houseboat vacation at Lake Powell. On Saturday night she called me to say she needed "bodies" for a scrapbooking party the next day, which would be the day before we were both leaving the country. I had so much to do but I could not turn her down.

Before I left her house Nancy gave me a piece of paper that had a distinctive scroll design and a story called, "The Tootsie Roll Ritual." I read it as she commented, "It reminded me of you." The story brought tears of remembrance of a grandmother who always carried a purse stuffed with candy bars. As we hugged, harder than I ever remember, she said, "I love you." "Me, too, you," I confided. We had never spoken those words to each other before. "Why, now," I wondered. We wished each other a good time and a safe trip as I left.

At the end of my third week in Costa Rica I received an urgent call from my husband. "Come home! Nancy was killed in a boating accident." He arranged a flight and I came home in a daze to bury my sister. David died eleven days later, leaving two small children to be raised by his sister.

Later, I framed the "Tootsie Roll Ritual" and hung it next to Nancy and David's picture. I was sure the story had come from a book so I always searched for it, always on the lookout for the recognizable scroll design, trying to find some link to her, but it always eluded me.

On Mother's Day, one and one half years later, Nancy's children gave me an unexpected gift. They waited anxiously for me to open the gift they had chosen on their own, without help. It was a book, *Chocolate for a Woman's Soul*. As I flipped through the pages the scroll work leaped out. I searched the index, and there it was: "The Tootsie Roll Ritual." Nancy's children couldn't have known. I had told no one. I miss her so much, but I know that somehow, she was guiding their choice, trying to let me know she is with us always.

Sincerely,
Merilee Glick

I sat at my desk and cried. For Merilee Glick to gain comfort from my story, I had to relinquish ownership and let go of my desire to be in control of exactly how my work unfolded. To participate in a small miracle, I had to join forces with another woman. I could not have possibly controlled any of the events. Partnering with Kay brought a woman I'd never met intense joy, and it gave me just as much. I took this fax as a huge message from my Creator: "Hey, I sent you down there with a mission to help people connect with what's really important. Sometimes you seem overwhelmed with the assignment. I've noticed you occasionally being territorial about your work. Did you honestly think I meant you were supposed to do your mission *alone*?"

> The universe multiplies our powers when we let go and embrace other women. Just like everything else in life, we have to give in order to receive. The lesson comes back to us over and over. We gain power by giving up control. How could you go easy on your territorial tendencies and pair up to power up?

Reach Out to Women

What if we refocused our energy to help each other become even more powerful? What if we reached out to women and said, "Together we are stronger." I spoke with Andrea Levin, a woman who celebrated her fiftieth birthday by inviting fifty of the most powerful women she knew to her party. Imagine the energy in *that* room! Think about the resources they could share, the beliefs they had in common, and the myriad ways they could challenge, stretch, and help each other grow.

What if we each helped another woman make her dream come true? Lynn Price fulfilled her dream when she founded Camp to Belong, a national nonprofit organization dedicated to reuniting brothers and sisters who are separated in foster care. The camp brings the biological siblings together for an unforgettable week of memory making. I serve as the national spokesperson, my daughter Emily spends her summer as a camp counselor, and my daughter Sarah donates her time to the fund-raising efforts. Helping Lynn with her vision has enriched my entire family. Do you know a woman with a vision who would love some help? Charlene Ferguson heads Sista's in the Spirit, a one-woman lending library of self-help books she has collected from garage sales, second-hand stores, and donations. Three Saturdays each month, she sets up her library at a Denver-area hair salon. She lends the books to women who need help the way she did years before when she survived turbulent personal problems. Are you familiar with Dress for Success, an international organization that collects and distributes your no-longer-needed business suits to lower-income women reentering the workforce? Dress for Success addresses the Catch-22 that without a job, how can you afford a suit? But without a suit, how can you get the job?

Have you heard of Anita Borg, long an advocate of women in computing, who started Systers List, a mailing list for women in technology? She created the Grace Hopper Celebration of Women in Computing, the first technical conference for women. Her nonprofit organization, Institute for Women and Technology, now serves women worldwide. Brenda Abdilla, an entrepreneur and mother, founded a Web site, ExpectantProfessional.com, because of her desire to help women reduce the anxiety and internal conflict that many career women feel about pregnancy and motherhood. Dr. Marie Savard, author of *How to Save Your Own Life*, has dedicated her career to helping women find the power to avoid the pitfalls of modern medicine and get the best health care possible. Dr. Savard believes "it will take women to transform health care, from the bottom up and one person at a time." These visionary women and millions more like them need our support to make their contributions to the world.

As I was writing this chapter, I received an e-mail from a woman who was about to celebrate her fifty-fifth birthday. She asked her friends to celebrate by donating to one of her favorite causes. She recommended the Heifer Project International. Its mission is to reduce hunger and poverty for recipients by buying them a flock of ducks, geese, or chicks ($20), a goat, pig, or sheep ($120), bees ($30), tree seedlings

($60), and, yes, even heifers ($500). In a form of "pay it forward," the recipient gives the animals' offspring to others. If you are feeling really flush you can buy an entire ark for $5,000. Her other recommendation was the Women for Women International project, which focuses on giving women the tools and resources they need to move out of crisis and poverty toward a life of stability and self-sufficiency. It tells women who have gone through terrible circumstances (for example, in Bosnia, Kosovo, Nigeria, or Rwanda) that they aren't forgotten and there is support to rebuild their lives. Women receive funds to seed their (mostly craft-related) businesses. Payback is 99.7 percent.

I love to think of the women and children worldwide who have benefited from the simple microaction of this e-mail. (For more information on these visionary women and their causes or businesses, see Resources for Powerful Women at the end of this book.)

What if we all committed to doing something every day to boost another woman up? Smile at her when she nurses in public. Refer business to a new entrepreneur. Pass on a compliment. Recommend her for a promotion. Take an extra carpool turn. Buy her a book. Invite her to go for a jog. Send an e-mail of thanks or congratulations. Tell her the truth. Step in when the babysitter cancels. Praise her for a job well done or for just being in your life. Tell her to go for a checkup. Mend a fence. Ask for her forgiveness. Listen to a teenage girl, a tired mother, or a lonely elder.

What if we found a mentor and became one ourselves? My wise and sensitive mentor, Roswitha Smale, has given me so much wonderful guidance. She told me that when faced with a decision, she asks herself, "Does this nurture my ego or my soul?" She told me both of them need nurturing, but as she matures, her goal is to tip the scales in favor of her soul. She lives passionately and productively for part of the year in the United States and then slowly and richly in France for the rest, bringing me perspectives on both the benefits of doing and the delights in just being.

What if women decided to come together, as John Lennon suggested, and give peace a chance? In my own city of Denver, thirteen women from Belfast, Ireland—seven Catholic and six Protestant—spent eleven days building five houses for single mothers as part of a Habitat for Humanity "Women Building a Legacy" project. The women, age twenty to fifty-one, are mothers, grandmothers, housewives, community workers, secretaries, and shop managers. Half had never traveled outside the United Kingdom or Ireland before this trip. Anne Carson, a Protestant, said working side by side brought the women closer. Maureen Brady, a Catholic, said, "I want to tell other women what can happen when we work together. Tell them how much we have in common." Let these women, who live geographically close but are worlds apart after more than than thirty years of sectarian conflict, hatred and mistrust, remind us of the peace, energy and reconciliation that is possible when women unite.

Find a way to reach out to other women. Help them with their visions; do something every day to boost a woman up; find a mentor and become one too. Pair up to create peace. Surround yourself with powerful women.

We Yearn for Connection

Each year I organize a charity event called Camp Out Under the Chandeliers. Women invite their sisters (or someone they wish was their sister) to an overnight "camp" at a luxury hotel. We make a craft project, have an ugly-bathrobe contest and a fashion clinic, and eat mashed potatoes out of martini glasses. We laugh and cry, sing around the "campfire," drink wine, and do African drumming to candlelight. The following morning, most of the attendees reappear bleary-eyed, begging me for coffee, because they stayed up into the wee hours of the morning talking with their bunkmates.

The event allows the "campers" to experience the closeness and magic that the foster children feel when they attend

Camp to Belong with their biological siblings. I am always thrilled that we raise a lot of money so we can reunite even more children. But I am most moved when I see the hunger that women have to share a bond with each other, to let down their guard and listen to each other's stories. I watch with delight as they rediscover how much they like partnering with women who seem to understand just what they're feeling. The energy created in the room is palpable, and the connections they create are long lasting.

When I witness this power of pairing up, my own commitment to help women is renewed. I know that if I could start my life over, I would double my efforts to support other women the second time around. I would boost them up more, teach them what I know, tap into their knowledge, and enjoy their success. I would realize that making them more powerful makes me more powerful in the long run. I would understand that there is no shortage of phenomenal women and no limit to what we can accomplish together.

TOOLS FOR YOUR REPAIR KIT
Pair Up!

1. Form an alliance to help you let go of your desire to control life's uncontrollables.

2. Defend another woman.

3. Become sabotage savvy.

4. Ease up on your territorial tendencies.

5. Reach out to women.

POWER UP!
In Real Life

Dear Mary,

I served as the president of the Children's Diabetes Guild this year. Twenty years ago, my friend Jill Behr asked me to join the guild. It was just starting its second year and was forming committees for the third Carousel Ball. It was a very exciting time in Denver, as the ball was a huge star-studded event.

It was January 1980, and we went to a kickoff luncheon at the home of Barbara Davis. She told us how her nine-year-old daughter had been diagnosed with diabetes two years before. As we left, Barbara gave each person a pink rose and said, "Thank you for caring; thank you for sharing your time." I picked up a brochure about juvenile diabetes because I wanted to learn more about the disease, and I wondered about my hostess's courage in coping with the challenge of caring for an ill daughter. Reading the brochure, I realized the symptoms for diabetes were those I saw in our youngest child, our nine-year-old son, Kevin.

I called our pediatrician. He assured me our son had had a urinalysis at his last physical in August and not to worry. He did not have diabetes, he told me. Six weeks went by, and on March 16, 1980, our son was in the children's ward at University Hospital. Had I not attended that luncheon, I would have failed to recognize the symptoms, and our child would have been at home that night instead of in the hospital. His blood sugar had reached extremely high levels, and he may not have awakened from a diabetic coma.

The next day I sent Barbara Davis a single pink rose with a note that said, "Thank you for caring, thank you for sharing your time. Today we have a son." I remember the florist asking if I wanted to send a dozen. I replied, "It takes only one to save a child." One friend asking another to volunteer. I wanted to tell you, Mary, that partnering with another woman saved my child's life.

Sincerely,

Gretchen Pope

A HOT FLASH OF POWER

Partner with women. Together we make a difference. Our strength is in our unity.

THREE

All Fixed Up

10

CONCLUSION
Powerful Women

Dear Readers,

I hope you have enjoyed exploring the concepts of power and control and the roles they play in your life. I wrote this book to help us understand what we do to block our energy and how we can open ourselves up to get more of what we want and need. Getting a handle on life is not possible, and even if it were, it's not the answer to our too-much-to-do-not-enough-time-to-do-it problems. Powering up, letting go of control so that energy will flow to us, is the solution. My fervent wish is that I have given you enough things to think about so you can let go and *then do everything with your power.*

In summary, here are your Hot Flashes of Power:

1. Pause before you judge. You'll save yourself and others *untold* misery.

2. Pay attention. Listen with your eyes, give from your heart, and stage a sit-in.

3. Pose good questions. Ask the right ones and reap the rewards.

4. Predict your Achilles' heel. You will turn your weakness into your strength and your failure into success.

5. Position yourself. Place your mind, body, and soul in the best possible position to receive all the abundance the universe has to offer.

6. Partner with women. Together we make a difference. Our strength is in our unity.

Thank you for taking this journey with me. At the beginning of this book, I told you that the world needs you. I hope you realize just how powerful you are. Katie, *open* the door, here we come!

Warmly,

Mary LoVerde

I WOULD LOVE
TO HEAR FROM YOU!

I would be delighted to know how you feel about control and how you use your power. Please send me your ideas, stories, insights, and feedback. Reach me at:

Mary LoVerde, M.S., A.N.P.
Life Balance, Inc.
12262 E. Villanova Dr.
Aurora, CO 80014
303-755-5806
connect597@aol.com
www.maryloverde.com

If you would like to be on Mary LoVerde's mailing list for a newsletter or E-zine please sign up on the Web site or mail or fax the following information:

Name: _____

Company: _____

Title: _____

Address: _____

State: _____

Postal code: _____

Country: _____

Telephone: _____

Fax: _____

E-mail address: _____

☐ Please contact me about having Mary speak at my
   company's or association's event.

Comments:

RESOURCES FOR POWERFUL WOMEN

I encourage you to contact these wonderful organizations. Please tell them I sent you.

Mary LoVerde: To inquire about speaking services or Life Balance books and products, go to www.maryloverde.com or e-mail: connect597@aol.com or call 303-755-5806. Autographed copies of this book, as well as of *Stop Screaming at the Microwave!* and *Touching Tomorrow,* are available.

Better Sleep Council: For a free copy of the Better Sleep Guide, write to the Better Sleep Council, Guide, P.O. Box 19534 Alexandria, VA 22320-0534 or e-mail: bsc@sleepproducts.org, or go to www.bettersleep.org, or call 703-683-8371.

Brenda Abdilla: To learn about practical strategies for business women during pregnancy, go to www.ExpectantProfessional.com, or call 303-424-1749.

Karyn Buxman: To subscribe to the biweekly e-zine LyteBytes, containing tips and resources on how to find humor in your personal and professional life, send an e-mail to Subscribe-LyteBytes @humorx.com. It's a free benefit. Call 573-221-9086.

Camp to Belong: To learn more about reuniting the biological siblings of foster children, to volunteer, or to sponsor a child at camp, go to www.Camptobelong.org, or call 303-791-0915. You may also learn how you can attend Camp Out Under the Chandeliers.

Dress for Success: To donate suits for women in need, go to www.DressforSuccess.org. Check your phone book for local listings.

Heifer Project International: To help families own their own animals, go to www.heifer.org, or call 800-422-0474.

Institute for Women and Technology: To learn about this nonprofit organization, inquire about seminars, or sign up on the Systers List, go to www. iwt.org, or call 650-812-4496.

International Habitat for Humanity: To donate or inquire about participating in home building, go to www.habitat.org, or look for Habitat for Humanity in your local phone book.

Miraval Spa: To inquire about services or the Equine Experience, call 1-800-825-4000, or go to www.miravalresort.com.

Roger von Oech: To inquire about creativity seminars, go to www.creativethink.com, or call 650-321-6775. Look for *Creative Whack Pack* in bookstores.

Dr. Marie Savard: To learn how you can become a more powerful consumer in the health care system, go to www.drsavard.com, or call 877-SAVARDS (728-2737).

Annette Simmons: To learn more about Group Process Consulting, which offers short, intense, emotionally anchored experiences in the form of speeches and workshops, go to groupprocessconsulting.com, or call 336-275-4404.

Sista's in the Spirit: For information about Charlene Ferguson and her self-help lending library or to donate books, write to cyferguson@qwest.net, or call 303-371-8854.

Women for Women International: To help women get back on their financial feet, go to www.womenforwomen.org, or call 202-737-7705.

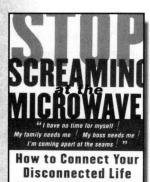
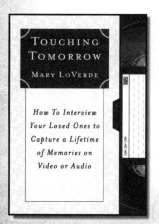